Stock Market as bedtime stories

Upon a Stock Market...

Mary Gracy

Foreword

As a veteran investor, I know firsthand how intimidating the stock market can seem to those who are just starting out. The financial jargon, technical terms, and complex calculations can make it seem like an impenetrable fortress of knowledge that only the elite can access. But that couldn't be further from the truth. The stock market is not just for the rich or the well-educated. It's a fascinating and dynamic ecosystem that anyone can learn to navigate with the right guidance.

That's why I was thrilled to read "Stock Market as Bedtime Stories", a delightful collection of narratives that simplifies the stock market basics in an engaging and accessible way. The book's author, [insert author name], has done a masterful job of crafting tales that weave together real-life investing principles with imaginative storytelling. Each story takes the reader on a journey through the stock market, introducing key concepts like diversification, risk management, and long-term investing in a way that's both entertaining and educational.

What I love most about this book is that it makes the stock market approachable to a wide range of readers. Whether you're a child who's just starting to learn about finances, a beginner investor who's looking to dip their toes in the water, or an experienced pro who's looking for a fresh perspective, "Stock Market as Bedtime Stories" has something to offer. The stories are relatable, the characters are endearing, and the lessons are valuable.

One of the things that makes investing so rewarding is the sense of empowerment that comes from taking control of your financial future. When you learn to invest wisely, you're not just making money, you're also gaining the confidence and independence that come from knowing how to manage your finances. "Stock Market as Bedtime Stories" is a wonderful resource for anyone who wants to develop that sense of financial literacy and take control of their financial future.

But the value of this book goes beyond just teaching financial literacy. It also encourages creativity, imagination, and critical thinking. By presenting the stock market as a world of adventure and discovery, it inspires readers to think outside the box and look at investing in a new light. The stories show that investing is not just about making money, it's also about understanding the world around us, predicting trends, and making informed decisions.

In a world where financial literacy is still woefully lacking, "Stock Market as Bedtime Stories" is a much-needed breath of fresh air. It shows that investing doesn't have to be dry or boring. It can be exciting, engaging, and fun. And when we make investing fun, we make it accessible to everyone.

I highly recommend "Stock Market as Bedtime Stories" to anyone who wants to learn about the stock market in a creative and imaginative way. Whether you're a parent who wants to teach your child about finances, an educator who wants to incorporate financial literacy into your curriculum, or just someone who's curious about investing, this book is for you. It's a testament to the power of storytelling and the importance of making investing accessible to everyone.

So sit back, relax, and let the stories in "Stock Market as Bedtime Stories" transport you to a world of financial wonder. Who knows, you may just learn something along the way.

Financial markets

Once upon a time, there was a small village named Marketville. The people in Marketville were very hardworking and always had something to sell, whether it was fruits, vegetables, or handcrafted items.

One day, a wise old man came to Marketville and told the people about a magical place called the Financial Market. He explained that it was a place where people could buy and sell different things, just like in their village, but on a much larger scale.

At first, the people of Marketville were confused. They didn't understand why someone would want to buy something from a stranger who lived far away. But the wise old man explained that there were many things that people needed that couldn't be found in their village.

He said that there were people who made things like clothes, toys, and machines, and they needed money to continue making these things. So, they would sell parts of their businesses, called "stocks," to people who believed in their work and wanted to help them succeed.

The people of Marketville were amazed! They realized that they too could buy these stocks and help these businesses grow. And if the businesses did well, the value of their stocks would increase, and they could sell them for a profit.

So, the people of Marketville started to participate in the Financial Market, buying and selling stocks of different businesses.

Some businesses did really well, and the people who invested in them became very wealthy. Other businesses didn't do as well, and the people who invested in them lost some of their money.

But overall, the people of Marketville learned that the Financial Market was a place where people could come together to invest in each other's dreams and help businesses grow. And that's how they learned about financial markets!

✼✼✼✼✼✼✼✼✼✼✼✼✼✼✼✼✼✼✼✼✼✼

Once upon a time, there was a young boy named Tim who loved collecting things. He had a collection of coins, stamps, and even rocks he found on his adventures.

One day, Tim's dad took him to a place called the Financial Market. Tim didn't know what it was, but he was excited to see if he could find something new to add to his collection.

When they arrived, Tim saw a big building with people walking in and out, carrying papers and talking on phones. His dad explained that it was a place where people could buy and sell different things, including pieces of ownership in companies, called stocks.

Tim was confused. "Why would someone want to buy a piece of a company?" he asked.

"Well," said his dad, "when you buy a stock, you become a part owner of that company. And if the company does well, the value of your stock goes up, and you can sell it for more money than you paid for it."

Tim was intrigued. He asked his dad if they could buy some stocks together. They went to a broker and bought a few shares in a company that made video games, which Tim loved to play.

Over time, Tim and his dad watched as the value of their stocks went up and down, depending on how well the company was doing. They learned that the financial market was a place where people could invest in companies they believed in, and help those companies grow.

Tim started to research different companies, looking for ones that he thought would do well. He discovered a company that made solar panels, and he thought it would be a great investment since it was good for the environment.

He convinced his dad to invest some money in that company, and over time, the value of their stocks went up as the company grew and became more successful.

Tim learned that the financial market wasn't just a place for adults to buy and sell things, but it was also a place where he could invest in things he believed in and help make a difference in the world.

****

Once upon a time, there was a town called Prosperity. The people in Prosperity were hardworking and always looking for ways to improve their lives.

One day, a group of business owners came to the town square and announced that they were starting a new company. They needed money to get the company off the ground, so they invited the people of Prosperity to invest in their venture.

At first, the people were hesitant. They didn't want to risk their hard-earned money on a new and untested business. But the business owners explained that by investing in their company, the people of Prosperity would be helping to create new jobs and boost the local economy.

So, the people of Prosperity started investing in the company. They pooled their money together and bought shares of the company, which meant that they owned a small part of it.

Over time, the company grew and became very successful. The value of the shares went up, and the people who invested in it made a profit. Some of them used that money to invest in other companies, which also grew and became successful.

Before long, Prosperity became known as a hub of innovation and entrepreneurship. The financial market, where people could buy and sell shares of different companies, became a bustling center of activity.

People started to see that by investing in companies, they could help create new opportunities and build a stronger economy. They learned that the financial market wasn't just a place to buy and sell things, but it was also a way to invest in the future of their community.

And that's how the people of Prosperity learned about the financial market and the power of investing in their own future.

****

Once upon a time, there was a girl named Lily who loved to bake. She was always experimenting with new recipes and trying out different ingredients.

One day, Lily decided that she wanted to turn her love of baking into a business. She wanted to open a bakery and sell her delicious treats to the world.

But she quickly realized that starting a business was expensive. She needed money for equipment, ingredients, and a storefront. So, she decided to look into getting a loan from a bank.

When she went to the bank, she met with a loan officer who explained that the bank would give her the money she needed, but she would have to pay it back with interest over time.

Lily was hesitant. She didn't want to go into debt and be stuck paying back a loan for years. But the loan officer explained that there was another way she could get the money she needed.

He told her about the financial market, where people could invest in businesses they believed in. He explained that by selling shares of her bakery to investors, Lily could raise the money she needed without taking on debt.

Lily was intrigued. She had never heard of the financial market before, but she liked the idea of having people invest in her business and help it grow.

So, she decided to give it a try. She created a business plan and started looking for investors. She found a group of people who loved her baking and were excited about the idea of investing in her bakery.

Together, they formed a company and sold shares to other investors in the financial market. As the bakery grew and became more successful, the value of the shares went up, and the investors made a profit.

Lily was thrilled. She had been able to turn her dream of owning a bakery into a reality, and she had done it with the help of people who believed in her.

She learned that the financial market wasn't just a place for big companies to raise money. It was also a place where small businesses like hers could get the funding they needed to grow and thrive.

And that's how Lily learned about the financial market and the power of investing in new and innovative ideas.

****

Once upon a time, there was a little boy named Alex who loved to collect stickers. He had a huge collection of shiny, colorful stickers that he loved to trade with his friends.

One day, Alex decided he wanted to get a really special sticker that he didn't have yet. It was a rare and valuable sticker that he had been wanting for a long time.

But he didn't have enough stickers to trade for it. He needed to find a way to get more stickers, and fast!

That's when he heard about the "Sticker Trading Market". It was a place where people could trade their stickers with other people from all over the world.

So, Alex went to the Sticker Trading Market to see what he could do. He met lots of other sticker collectors who were looking for special stickers too.

Alex found a collector who had the sticker he wanted. The collector was willing to trade the sticker, but he wanted something really valuable in return.

Alex didn't have anything else to trade, but he really wanted that sticker. That's when he remembered something his mom had told him about the financial market.

She had explained that it was a place where people could buy and sell things, like stocks and bonds, to make money. She had also said that sometimes people could trade things they owned for other things they wanted.

So, Alex had an idea. He went back to the collector and offered to give him some of his allowance money in exchange for the special sticker.

The collector liked this idea, so they made the trade. Alex was so excited to finally have the sticker he had been wanting, and he had learned about the power of the financial market.

He realized that just like the Sticker Trading Market, there were other markets where people could trade things they owned for things they wanted. And that's how Alex learned about the financial market, all because of his love for collecting stickers!

Gross domestic product

Once upon a time, there was a group of friends who loved to play together. They would have picnics, play games, and go on adventures.

One day, they decided to build a fort in the backyard. They gathered all the materials they needed: blankets, pillows, and chairs.

As they built their fort, they realized they needed more blankets and pillows to make it bigger and more comfortable. So, they asked their parents for help.

The parents all agreed to pitch in and bring more blankets and pillows to the fort. Some parents brought snacks and drinks too.

As the group played in their fort, they realized that everyone had brought something to contribute. Each person's contribution made the fort bigger and better.

That's when one of the friends, named Sarah, said, "We should add up everything we brought and see how much our fort is worth!"

The group thought this was a great idea. They added up the value of all the blankets, pillows, chairs, snacks, and drinks. They were amazed at how much their fort was worth!

They realized that just like their fort, there was something called the Gross Domestic Product, or GDP, that added up the value of everything a country produced in a year.

They learned that just like their fort, the value of everything a country produced helped to show how well the country was doing.

The group was proud of their fort and proud to have learned about the Gross Domestic Product, all because of their love for building and playing together.

****

Once upon a time, there was a little girl named Lily who loved to bake cookies. She would bake cookies every week and give them to her family and friends.

One day, her mom asked her to bake some cookies for a school fundraiser. Lily was excited to help and decided to bake as many cookies as she could.

She went to the store to buy ingredients like flour, sugar, and chocolate chips. She spent a lot of time in the kitchen baking dozens and dozens of cookies.

When she brought the cookies to the school fundraiser, people loved them! They sold out quickly and raised a lot of money for the school.

Lily was proud of herself for making so many cookies and helping the school. But her mom explained to her that her cookies were not just helpful, they were also valuable.

She said that just like Lily's cookies, there were many things that people made and sold in a country. These things, like cars, clothes, and toys, were all added up to make something called Gross Domestic Product, or GDP.

Lily was curious and wanted to know more. Her mom explained that the GDP showed how much a country was making and how well the people in the country were doing.

Lily was happy to know that her cookies had helped to raise money for the school and also contributed to the GDP of the country.

From that day on, Lily continued to bake cookies and other treats, knowing that she was not only making people happy, but also contributing to the GDP of the country.

∗∗∗∗∗∗∗∗∗∗∗∗∗∗∗∗∗∗∗∗∗

Once upon a time, there was a little boy named Timmy who loved to play with toys. He had so many toys that he didn't know what to do with them all!

One day, Timmy's mom asked him to help her clean up his toys. Timmy was happy to help, but he didn't want to give any of his toys away.

Instead, he came up with a great idea. He decided to invite all his friends over to play with his toys. They played for hours and had so much fun.

As the day went on, Timmy's friends started to leave, and his mom came in to check on him. She saw all the toys scattered around the room and asked Timmy, "Do you know how much all these toys are worth?"

Timmy shook his head, not understanding what his mom meant. So, she explained to him that all the toys he had in his room were like the things that people make and sell in a country. And just like his toys, all those things added up to something called Gross Domestic Product, or GDP.

Timmy didn't fully understand what his mom was talking about, but he knew that his toys were valuable to him. He loved playing with them and sharing them with his friends.

And that's what GDP is all about – the things that people make and sell that are valuable to them and to others. Timmy may have been young, but he learned that everything has value and contributes to the world around us.

****

Once upon a time, there was a little girl named Emma who loved to draw and color pictures. She would spend hours making pictures of flowers, animals, and her favorite cartoon characters.

One day, Emma's mom asked her if she could draw a picture to give to her grandma as a gift. Emma was excited and started to draw a beautiful picture of a butterfly.

When she finished the picture, Emma's mom told her that her drawing was very special and valuable. She explained that just like Emma's drawing, there were many things that people made and sold in a country, like toys, clothes, and food.

All these things were added up to make something called Gross Domestic Product, or GDP. GDP was a way to measure how well a country was doing, by seeing how much people were making and selling.

Emma was curious and wanted to know more, so her mom showed her some pictures of things that people made, like cars and houses. She told Emma that all these things added up to make the GDP of the country.

Emma was happy to know that her drawing was not just a gift for her grandma, but it was also a part of the GDP of the country. She continued to draw and color pictures, knowing that they were valuable and contributed to the world around her.

****

Once upon a time, there was a little boy named Jack who loved to play with his toy trucks and cars. He would make them zoom around the room and race against each other.

One day, Jack's dad came home from work and showed him a big box of cookies that he had made at his job. Jack's dad worked at a bakery, and he told Jack that the cookies were going to be sold to people who loved sweets.

Jack was excited to try a cookie, but he didn't understand why his dad was so happy about making them. His dad explained that when people bought the cookies, it helped his job and the bakery to earn money.

And when many people bought cookies, it added up to something called Gross Domestic Product, or GDP. GDP was like a big scoreboard that showed how much money all the people in the country were making from selling things like cookies, toys, clothes, and even cars and houses.

Jack thought that was really cool, and he decided to help his dad by handing out some of the cookies to their neighbors. When his dad's boss found out, he was really happy and said that Jack's help was like a bonus cookie that added to the GDP of the bakery and the country.

From that day on, Jack understood that everything people made and sold, even cookies, was important and contributed to the world around him.

****

Once upon a time, there was a little girl named Lily who loved to play with her friends at the park. They would swing on the swings, climb on the jungle gym, and slide down the slide.

One day, a new playground was built in the park, and Lily was so excited to play on it. She asked her mom how it got there, and her mom told her that the city built it using money from taxes.

Lily was curious and wanted to know more about where the money came from. Her mom explained that when people worked at their jobs and earned money, they paid some of it to the government as taxes.

All the money that the government collected from taxes and spent on things like playgrounds, schools, and hospitals was added up to something called Gross Domestic Product, or GDP. GDP was like a big calculator that showed how much all the people in the country were making and spending.

Lily thought that was really interesting, and she decided to thank her mom for working and paying taxes so that they could have a nice park to play in. Her mom smiled and said that everyone's hard work and contributions, even in small ways, added up to make the country a better place.

From that day on, Lily understood that the things she enjoyed, like the playground, were not just magically there, but they were a result of the hard work and cooperation of everyone in the country.

Gross National Product

Once upon a time, there was a little boy named Max who loved to help his mom in their small garden. They would plant seeds, water the plants, and watch them grow into beautiful flowers and delicious vegetables.

One day, Max's mom told him that they were going to sell some of their vegetables at the farmer's market in town. Max was excited and asked how much money they would get for them. His mom explained that the money they earned from selling the vegetables was like their own little Gross National Product, or GNP.

Max was confused and asked what Gross National Product meant. His mom told him that just like they grew things in their garden, many people worked and made things in their own countries. When they sold those things to people in other countries, it added up to the Gross National Product of their country.

Max thought that was really neat and asked if they could sell their vegetables to people in other countries. His mom laughed and said that their garden was too small, but there were many farmers in their country who sold their crops to other countries and helped to increase the GNP of their country.

From that day on, Max understood that the things his family and other people made and sold not only helped them earn money, but also helped to strengthen their country's economy and Gross National Product.

* * * * * * * * * * * * * * * * * * * *

Once upon a time, there was a little girl named Mia who loved to draw pictures with her crayons. She would draw flowers, animals, and her favorite cartoon characters.

One day, her mom saw her drawings and thought they were so beautiful that she decided to send some to her aunt who lived in another country. Mia was excited and asked how her aunt would get the pictures.

Her mom explained that there were big machines called planes that could fly people and things to other countries. When the pictures arrived, Mia's aunt would be very happy and might even show them to her friends. When people in other countries bought things that were made or designed in their country, it added up to the Gross National Product, or GNP.

Mia was fascinated and asked how they knew how much money the pictures were worth. Her mom told her that there were people called economists who studied how much things were worth and how much people were willing to pay for them.

From that day on, Mia understood that the things she made, even just her drawings, could contribute to her country's Gross National Product and help it grow stronger. She continued to draw and share her pictures with others, knowing that she was a part of something bigger than just her own drawings.

* * * * * * * * * * * * * * * * * * * *

Once upon a time, there was a little boy named Timmy who loved to play with his toy cars. He had a big collection of cars, trucks, and buses that he would play with every day.

One day, his mom asked him if he wanted to sell some of his toy cars at a garage sale. Timmy thought it was a great idea and asked how much money he could get for them.

His mom explained that the money they would earn from selling the toys was like their own Gross National Product, or GNP. She told Timmy that just like he had his own collection of toy cars, many people in their country made and sold things to people in other countries, and that added up to the Gross National Product of their country.

Timmy was surprised and asked if he could sell his toy cars to people in other countries. His mom explained that their garage sale was just for people in their neighborhood, but there were many stores in their country that sold toys to people in other countries and helped to increase the GNP of their country.

Timmy was happy to learn that even his toy cars could help to make their country's economy stronger. He decided to sell some of his toy cars and put the money in his piggy bank, knowing that he was contributing to something bigger than just his own collection of toys.

****

Once upon a time, there was a little girl named Lily who lived in a village with her family. The village had many farmers who grew fruits and vegetables that they sold at a market in town.

One day, Lily's family decided to start their own farm and grow their own fruits and vegetables. They worked hard every day to plant seeds, water the plants, and take care of their crops.

When their crops were ready, they took them to the market in town to sell. They sold so many fruits and vegetables that they had to go back to the farm and pick more. Lily was happy to see how much people loved their fruits and vegetables.

Her mom told her that the money they earned from selling their crops was like their own Gross National Product, or GNP. Lily was curious and asked what that meant.

Her mom explained that just like their family worked hard to grow their own crops, many other families in their country worked hard to make things that they sold to people in other countries. When all of those things were added up, it was called the Gross National Product, and it helped their country to become stronger and more prosperous.

Lily was proud to be a part of their country's Gross National Product and continued to work hard on their farm, knowing that she was contributing to something bigger than just their own family.

****

Once upon a time, there was a little boy named Max who loved to draw and color. He had a big box of crayons and would spend hours making colorful drawings.

One day, Max's mom asked him if he wanted to sell some of his drawings at a community fair. Max was excited and asked how much money he could get for them.

His mom explained that the money they would earn from selling Max's drawings was like their own Gross National Product, or GNP. She told Max that just like he had his own collection of drawings, many people in their country made and sold things to people in other countries, and that added up to the Gross National Product of their country.

Max was surprised and asked if he could sell his drawings to people in other countries. His mom explained that the fair was just for people in their community, but there were many stores in their country that sold artwork to people in other countries and helped to increase the GNP of their country.

Max was happy to learn that even his drawings could help to make their country's economy stronger. He decided to sell some of his drawings and put the money in his piggy bank, knowing that he was contributing to something bigger than just his own artwork.

****

Once upon a time, there was a little girl named Emma who loved to play with her toys. She had a lot of toys that she had collected over the years and she loved to share them with her friends.

One day, Emma's mom told her that they were going to have a garage sale and that they could sell some of her toys to make some extra money. Emma was excited and asked how much money they could make.

Her mom explained that the money they would earn from selling Emma's toys was like their own Gross National Product, or GNP. She told Emma that just like they were selling toys, many people in their country made and sold things to people in other countries, and that added up to the Gross National Product of their country.

Emma was interested and asked what kinds of things people in their country made and sold to other countries. Her mom explained that there were many things like cars, clothes, and electronics that were made in their country and sold to people all over the world.

Emma was happy to learn that even her toys could help to make their country's economy stronger. She decided to pick out some of her toys to sell and put the money in her piggy bank, knowing that she was contributing to something bigger than just her own toys.

****

Once upon a time, there was a little boy named Jake who loved to go to the park and play on the swings and slides. One day, he noticed that there were a lot of other kids at the park too, and they were all playing with different toys and games.

Jake's mom told him that all of those toys and games were made by people in their country, just like the food they ate and the clothes they wore. She explained that when people in their country made and sold things to people in other countries, it helped to make their country's Gross National Product, or GNP, stronger.

Jake was curious and asked how he could help to make the GNP stronger. His mom suggested that he could start a lemonade stand in the park and sell cups of lemonade to the other kids. Jake loved the idea and got to work making a big pitcher of lemonade.

When he was ready, he set up his lemonade stand and started selling cups of lemonade to the other kids in the park. Soon, he had made a lot of money and put it all in his piggy bank. His mom explained that the money he earned from selling lemonade was like a small part of their country's GNP, and that everyone could do their part to help make it stronger.

Jake was proud to have helped make his country's economy stronger, even if it was just a little bit. From that day on, he continued to look for ways to contribute to his country's GNP, and he always remembered the fun he had selling lemonade in the park.

****

Once upon a time, there was a little girl named Lily who loved to draw and color. She would spend hours every day making beautiful pictures with her crayons and markers. One day, her mom came into her room and saw all the drawings Lily had made.

"Lily," said her mom, "you're so talented! You know, every time you make a picture, it helps to make our country's Gross National Product, or GNP, stronger."

Lily didn't understand what her mom meant, so her mom explained that when people in their country made and sold things, it helped to make the country's economy stronger. And when Lily made a picture, it was like she was creating something that people might want to buy, which helped to make the country's GNP stronger.

Lily was excited to know that her drawings could help make the country's economy stronger. She asked her mom if they could sell her pictures to people. Her mom suggested that they could have an art show and invite people to come see Lily's drawings.

So, Lily and her mom worked hard to organize an art show in their community center. They put up posters all over town, and on the day of the show, lots of people came to see Lily's drawings. Some people even bought her pictures to hang on their walls at home.

Lily was so happy to have made a contribution to her country's economy. She felt proud of her talent and was grateful that her drawings could help make a difference. From that day on, she continued to make beautiful pictures, knowing that each one was helping to make her country stronger.

Difference Between Gdp and Gnp

Once upon a time, there was a group of friends who loved to play together. There was Timmy, Sarah, and their friend Alex. They loved playing games, and they decided to start a lemonade stand to earn some money.

One day, Timmy and Sarah decided to count all the money they had made from their lemonade stand. They counted the money they earned by selling lemonade to their friends, and they also counted the money they earned by selling lemonade to people who were visiting their town from other countries.

Alex noticed that Timmy and Sarah had counted the money they earned from visitors, and he asked them why. They explained to Alex that they were counting all the money they earned, whether it was from their friends or visitors from other countries.

Alex then explained that the money they earned from visitors from other countries was part of the Gross National Product or GNP, while the money they earned from their friends was part of the Gross Domestic Product or GDP.

The children were confused and asked Alex to explain what he meant. Alex said that GDP is the total amount of money earned in a country by all the people who live there, including children like themselves. But GNP is the total amount of money earned by everyone who lives in a country, including people who live in other countries but earn money from the country.

The children were still a bit confused, so Alex decided to give them an example. He said that if their lemonade stand was the entire country, then the money they earned from their friends would be GDP, while the money they earned from visitors from other countries would be GNP.

Timmy, Sarah, and Alex were happy to have learned something new, and they continued to run their lemonade stand, knowing that their earnings were part of the country's GDP and GNP.

****

Once upon a time, there were two neighboring villages. In one village, everyone worked hard to make things and sell them to each other. In the other village, some people made things and sold them to people in their own village, but others made things and sold them to people in the neighboring village.

One day, a wise old owl came to visit the villages and taught them about Gross Domestic Product (GDP) and Gross National Product (GNP). The owl explained that GDP is the total amount of money made by the people who live in a country or village. So, in the first village, the GDP would be the total amount of money made by everyone who lived there, by selling things to each other.

But GNP is the total amount of money made by everyone who lives in a country, no matter where they make it. So, in the second village, the GNP would include the money made by people who sold things to the neighboring village, even if they didn't live there.

The owl then asked the villagers if they could think of any examples of things that people in the second village might make and sell to the neighboring village. One person said, "What about honey?

We have a lot of bees and make a lot of honey, and the neighboring village doesn't have any bees."

The owl smiled and said, "Yes, that's a great example. The people who make and sell honey to the neighboring village would be contributing to the GNP of both villages, because even though they live in one village, they are making money from people in the other village."

The villagers were excited to have learned something new, and they thanked the wise old owl for his visit. From then on, they knew that GDP and GNP were important ways of measuring the amount of money made by people, both in their own village and in the neighboring villages.

✶✶✶✶✶✶✶✶✶✶✶✶✶✶✶✶✶✶✶✶

Once upon a time, there was a little girl named Lily who lived in a village. She loved playing with her friends and helping her parents in their small shop. One day, her teacher came to the class and asked them if they knew the difference between GDP and GNP.

Lily raised her hand and asked, "What are GDP and GNP, teacher?" The teacher explained that GDP is like the money made by all the people who live in the village, and GNP is like the money made by all the people who live in the village plus the money made by people from other villages who sell things to the people in Lily's village.

Lily thought about it for a moment and then asked, "So, if my mom and dad sell things to people in our village, that's GDP, right?" The teacher nodded and said, "Yes, that's correct. But if your mom and dad also sell things to people in other villages, then that's part of GNP."

Lily still didn't quite understand, so her teacher decided to explain it with an example. She asked, "Do you know where the delicious apples we eat come from?" Lily shook her head, so the teacher explained that some apples come from farms in their own village, while others come from farms in neighboring villages.

"So," the teacher continued, "if people from other villages come to our village to sell their apples, then that money they make from selling their apples would be included in the GNP, because they're not from our village. But if someone from our own village sells their apples to someone else in our village, then that would be part of the GDP."

Lily smiled and said, "Oh, I get it now! So, GDP is like all the money made in our own village, and GNP is like all the money made in our village plus the money made by people from other villages who sell things to us."

Her teacher smiled and said, "Exactly! You're very smart, Lily." From then on, Lily was proud to know the difference between GDP and GNP, and she was excited to tell her parents all about it when she got home from school.

****

Once upon a time, there were two cousins, GDP and GNP. They both loved playing with toys and having fun. GDP lived in a big city and GNP lived in a small town. One day, they decided to have a toy trading party.

GDP brought toys that were made in his city, like toy cars and robots. GNP brought toys that were made in his town, like toy horses and farm sets. They started to trade their toys with each other, but soon they realized that they had a problem. The toys that were made in GDP's city were too big for GNP's town, and the toys that were made in GNP's town were too small for GDP's city.

That's when they came up with an idea. They decided to trade based on where the toys were made, not on their size. This made the trading fair and fun for both of them. GDP realized that even though his city made big and cool toys, GNP's town had unique and special toys too. GNP realized that even though his town made small and simple toys, GDP's city had amazing and advanced toys too.

In the end, they both had a lot of fun playing with each other's toys and learning about the different things that their cities and towns were good at making. They realized that just like their toy trading party, GDP and GNP are both important in measuring how well their countries are doing. GDP measures the value of all the things made in a country, no matter who makes them, while GNP measures the value of all the things made by people from a particular country, no matter where they are made.

From that day on, GDP and GNP played together often, and they never forgot the important lesson they learned about fairness and equality.

Relation between GDP and GNP

Once upon a time, there were two friends named GDP and GNP. They lived in a big city with many other friends who were also important.

One day, GDP and GNP were playing a game called "The Economy Game." In this game, they had to help each other by exchanging different things, like toys or candy.

GDP was very good at producing things. He had a toy factory where he made lots of different toys that other friends loved to play with. On the other hand, GNP had a lot of money, which he used to buy things from other friends and help them start their own businesses.

One day, while playing the game, they realized that they were very dependent on each other. GDP needed GNP's money to buy raw materials and pay his workers to make toys. And GNP needed GDP's toys to sell to other friends and make a profit.

They learned that if one of them did not do well, it would affect the other one. For example, if GNP did not have enough money to buy toys from GDP, GDP's toy factory would not make as much money, and his workers might have to stop working. This would also affect other friends who relied on GDP's toys.

Similarly, if GDP did not make good toys, GNP would not be able to sell them to other friends and would not make as much profit. This would affect his ability to buy more toys from GDP and help other friends start their businesses.

So, they both realized that they needed to work together and help each other out to be successful in the game. And this is why GDP is dependent on GNP, as they both play a crucial role in helping each other and other friends in the economy.

The end.

****

Once upon a time, there were two neighboring kingdoms, the Kingdom of Goods and the Kingdom of Services. The Kingdom of Goods was famous for producing delicious fruits and vegetables, while the Kingdom of Services was famous for providing excellent medical care.

One day, the king of the Kingdom of Goods decided to open a hospital in his kingdom, as he saw that many of his people were getting sick and needed medical attention. The king of the Kingdom of Services was happy to help and sent his best doctors and nurses to the Kingdom of Goods.

The doctors and nurses worked hard and helped many people in the Kingdom of Goods to get better. This made the people of the Kingdom of Goods very happy, and they started to spend more money on other things like food and clothes. This increase in spending led to an increase in the Kingdom of Goods' GDP, as the goods produced in the kingdom were being sold more.

However, the doctors and nurses who were sent from the Kingdom of Services were being paid by their own kingdom. This meant that the money they earned was not counted as a part of the Kingdom of Goods' GDP. Instead, it was added to the Kingdom of Services' GNP as it was money earned by their citizens outside of their kingdom.

So, even though the Kingdom of Goods' GDP was increasing due to the increase in spending, it was still dependent on the Kingdom of Services' GNP, as the money earned by the doctors and nurses was being counted towards the GNP of the Kingdom of Services.

In this way, the story of the two kingdoms teaches us that even though GDP and GNP are different, they are still connected. The money earned by citizens of one kingdom while working in another kingdom contributes to the GNP of their own kingdom, but it also affects the GDP of the kingdom they are working in.

****

Once upon a time, there were two neighboring towns called Happyland and Smileyville. Happyland was famous for its delicious fruits and vegetables, while Smileyville was known for its beautiful handicrafts.

One day, the people of Happyland decided to send their fruits and vegetables to Smileyville to sell. The people of Smileyville were happy to receive such fresh produce and began to sell them in their markets. The fruits and vegetables were so delicious that many people from other towns came to Smileyville to buy them.

As more and more people bought the fruits and vegetables, the market in Smileyville grew bigger and bigger. People began to make more money selling the produce and started spending more in the local shops. The shopkeepers in Smileyville were also happy as they were making more sales.

Soon, the people of Happyland realized that they could make even more money by selling their produce in Smileyville. They started to plant more fruits and vegetables and sent even more to Smileyville. As a result, the market in Smileyville continued to grow and the people of both towns became even happier.

This story shows how the growth of the market in Smileyville was dependent on the fresh produce from Happyland. In the same way, the Gross Domestic Product (GDP) of a country is dependent on the Gross National Product (GNP) of its citizens. The GDP of a country is the total value of all goods and services produced within the country's borders, while GNP is the total value of goods and services produced by a country's citizens, regardless of where they are located.

When the citizens of a country produce more and earn more money, they tend to spend more within the country's borders, leading to an increase in GDP. This is similar to how the people of Smileyville spent more money in their local shops when they earned more selling the fresh produce from Happyland.

In conclusion, the story of Happyland and Smileyville helps us understand how a country's GDP is dependent on the GNP of its citizens.

****

Once upon a time, there was a big family living in a village. They loved to make delicious food and sell it to their neighbors. They used their homegrown vegetables and spices to make the food and sold it for a small profit.

One day, the family decided to start selling their food to people outside of their village. They traveled to nearby towns and cities to sell their food. They found out that the people there loved their food too and were willing to pay more for it! The family was very happy because they were making more money than before.

But then, one day, a big storm came and destroyed all their vegetable crops. They didn't have enough food to sell and they started losing money. They couldn't travel to other towns to sell their food either because the storm had affected other areas too.

This is where GNP and GDP come in. GNP stands for Gross National Product, which means the total value of goods and services produced by a country's citizens, no matter where they are in the world. GDP stands for Gross Domestic Product, which means the total value of goods and services produced within a country's borders, regardless of who produced them.

Because the family was traveling to other towns and selling their food to people there, they were contributing to the GNP of their country. But when the storm hit and they couldn't sell their food anymore, their contribution to the GNP decreased. However, the family was still producing food within their own village, which contributed to the GDP of their country.

So you see, the GNP of a country depends on how much its citizens are producing and selling outside the country, while the GDP depends on how much they are producing within the country. And sometimes, one can affect the other, just like in the case of the family's food business.

****

Once upon a time, there was a village with many farmers who grew delicious fruits and vegetables. They worked hard every day to grow their crops and sell them to the nearby towns. One day, a group of travelers came to the village and offered to buy all the fruits and vegetables the farmers had grown.

The farmers were very excited and started working even harder to produce more fruits and vegetables. They were able to sell everything they produced and earned a lot of money. They used this money to buy better equipment and tools to grow even more crops.

But one day, a storm came and destroyed all the crops. The farmers were devastated because they had invested so much time and money into their farms. They didn't have anything to sell and couldn't earn any money.

That's when the travelers came back to the village and offered to help the farmers. They told them that they would buy the same amount of fruits and vegetables they had bought before, even if the farmers weren't able to produce as much because of the storm. The travelers also gave the farmers some money so they could buy new seeds and start growing crops again.

The farmers were very grateful and started working hard again. Even though they weren't able to produce as much as before because of the storm, they were still able to sell their crops and earn money. The travelers continued to buy from them and helped them out whenever they faced any difficulties.

In this story, the travelers represent the rest of the world that buys goods and services from a country. The farmers represent the businesses and workers in a country who produce goods and services. The storm represents any event, like a recession or a natural disaster, that can affect a country's economy.

When the travelers continued to buy from the farmers even though they produced less, it helped to maintain the farmers' income and their ability to invest in their farms. Similarly, when other countries continue to buy goods and services from a country even if their economy faces challenges, it helps to support that country's Gross Domestic Product (GDP).

GNP (Gross National Product) is similar to GDP, but it includes the income earned by a country's citizens and businesses abroad. So, a country's GDP is dependent on its own businesses and workers, while its GNP is also dependent on their activities abroad.

Relation between GDP, GNP and Financial market

Once upon a time, there was a town named Happyville. The people of Happyville were very hardworking and they loved to grow fruits and vegetables in their gardens. They would often share their fruits and vegetables with their neighbors, which made everyone very happy.

One day, the people of Happyville decided to sell their fruits and vegetables to other towns. They thought that by doing so, they could earn some extra money to buy things they needed. So, they decided to build a marketplace where they could sell their fruits and vegetables.

The marketplace became very popular, and people from all over the country came to buy fruits and vegetables from Happyville. This made the people of Happyville very happy because they were earning more money than they ever had before.

One day, a man named Mr. Moneybags came to Happyville. Mr. Moneybags was very rich and he wanted to invest his money in the town. He met with the mayor and said, "I have a lot of money and I want to invest it in your town. Can you tell me what your gross domestic product and gross national product are?"

The mayor was confused and did not know what Mr. Moneybags was talking about. Mr. Moneybags explained, "Gross domestic product (GDP) is the total value of all goods and services produced in a country in a year. Gross national product (GNP) is the total value of all goods and services produced by a country's citizens, even if they are living abroad, in a year."

The mayor realized that Happyville did not have a clear idea about its GDP and GNP. So, he asked Mr. Moneybags for help. Mr. Moneybags suggested that they could use the money earned from selling fruits and vegetables to invest in other businesses in Happyville. This would increase the town's GDP and GNP.

The mayor agreed, and they used the money to build factories that produced toys, clothes, and furniture. The people of Happyville worked hard in these factories and produced goods that were sold all over the country. This increased the town's GDP and GNP and made everyone even happier.

As the town's GDP and GNP increased, more people wanted to invest in Happyville. This led to the growth of a financial market, where people could invest their money in Happyville's businesses. This helped the businesses grow even more, which increased Happyville's GDP and GNP even further.

And so, Happyville continued to grow and prosper, thanks to the hard work of its people, their love for sharing, and the wise investments that increased its GDP and GNP.

****

Once upon a time, there was a big and bustling city called Econoville. In Econoville, there were many people who worked very hard every day to create and sell different things. They made toys, clothes, cars, and even food! All of these things were important to the people of Econoville, and they worked hard to make sure that they were the best they could be.

Now, there were three important things that the people of Econoville cared about: Gross Domestic Product, Gross National

Product, and the Financial Market. These might sound like big, complicated words, but they're really just a way of keeping track of how well Econoville is doing.

Gross Domestic Product (GDP) is like a big scoreboard that keeps track of how much money all the people and businesses in Econoville are making from selling their goods and services. The higher the number, the better Econoville is doing! But that's not the only thing that matters.

Gross National Product (GNP) is like another scoreboard that keeps track of all the money that Econoville's people and businesses make, even if they're selling things in other countries. This is important because it shows how much money Econoville is bringing in from all over the world.

And finally, there's the Financial Market. This is where people can buy and sell things like stocks and bonds, which are like little pieces of ownership in different companies. When a company does well and makes a lot of money, the value of those little pieces goes up, and people can sell them for more than they bought them for! It's like a big game, and people are always trying to win by buying and selling at just the right time.

But the thing is, all of these things are connected! When the people and businesses in Econoville are doing well and making lots of money, the GDP goes up. When the GDP goes up, it means that Econoville is doing well, and people want to invest in it. So the value of the things in the Financial Market goes up too!

And when the people and businesses in Econoville are making money all over the world, the GNP goes up. When the GNP goes up, it means that Econoville is bringing in lots of money from all over the world, and people want to invest in it even more. So the value of the things in the Financial Market goes up even more!

So you see, it's all connected! The better Econoville does, the more people want to invest in it, and the higher the value of the things in the Financial Market goes. It's like a big circle, and it keeps going around and around, making Econoville stronger and stronger.

And that's why everyone in Econoville works so hard to make sure they're doing their best!

Interest rates

Once upon a time, there was a boy named Johnny.

Johnny loved to save his allowance money to buy toys and candy. One day, his mother told him that if he saved his money in the bank, he could earn more money in the future.

Johnny was curious and asked his mother how that worked. His mother explained to him that the bank is like a big piggy bank for grown-ups, where people can deposit their money and earn extra money called "interest."

Johnny was intrigued and asked his mother, "What is interest?" His mother explained that interest is like a little reward for saving your money. If you save your money in the bank, the bank will give you extra money called "interest" on top of the money you saved.

Johnny was excited and asked his mother how much interest he could earn. His mother explained that the amount of interest you earn depends on the interest rate, which is set by the government.

Johnny was a bit confused and asked his mother what the government has to do with his piggy bank. His mother explained that the government sets the interest rate to help the economy grow. When the economy is doing well, the government will lower the interest rate to encourage people to borrow money and spend it, which helps businesses make more money and create jobs. But when the economy is not doing well, the government will raise the interest rate to encourage people to save their money instead of spending it, which helps stabilize the economy.

Johnny was fascinated by this and decided to save his money in the bank so he could earn interest and help the economy grow. He learned that interest rates are an important tool that the government uses to keep the economy healthy and strong.

****

Once upon a time, there was a piggy bank named Penny who loved to save her money. She had a special spot in her room where she kept all her coins and bills. One day, she heard her parents talking about something called "interest rates."

Penny was curious, so she asked her parents what interest rates were. They explained that when people save their money in a bank, the bank gives them extra money for keeping their money there. This extra money is called interest. The amount of interest given depends on something called the interest rate.

Penny wanted to know more, so her parents gave her an example. They said, "Let's say you have 100 pennies in your piggy bank, and the bank is offering a 5% interest rate. That means if you keep your 100 pennies in the bank for a whole year, the bank will give you an extra 5 pennies for keeping your money with them."

Penny was excited about the idea of getting extra pennies, so she decided to put her money in the bank. But then her parents explained that sometimes the interest rate can change. If the interest rate goes up, she will get more extra pennies. But if it goes down, she will get fewer extra pennies.

Penny realized that interest rates were important because they could affect how much extra money she could earn. She learned that banks use interest rates to encourage people to save their money with them, and that the interest rates can be influenced by many things, such as how well the economy is doing or how much money the government has.

From that day on, Penny kept an eye on the interest rates and made sure to put her money in the bank when the interest rates were high. She loved watching her savings grow, and she knew that understanding interest rates helped her make the most of her money.

****

Once upon a time, there was a family who lived in a big house. The family had some extra money that they didn't need right away, so they decided to put it in a bank.

The bank was like a big piggy bank for grown-ups. The family gave the bank their money and the bank promised to keep it safe. In return for keeping the money safe, the bank paid the family a little bit of extra money every year. This little bit of extra money is called "interest."

Now, the bank needed to make some money too, so they would lend the money to other people who needed it, like people who wanted to buy a car or a house. The people who borrowed the money had to pay the bank back, but they also had to pay a little bit of extra money on top of what they borrowed. This little bit of extra money is also called "interest."

The amount of interest the bank pays the family and the amount of interest the bank charges people who borrow money depends on something called "interest rates." Interest rates are like the price of borrowing money.

If interest rates are low, it means it doesn't cost as much to borrow money, so more people will want to borrow money. This can be good for the economy because people are buying more things and businesses are making more money.

But if interest rates are too high, it means it costs a lot to borrow money, so fewer people will want to borrow money. This can slow down the economy because people aren't buying as much and businesses aren't making as much money.

So you see, interest rates are very important because they can affect how much money people can borrow, how much people can save, and how the economy is doing overall.

∗∗∗∗∗∗∗∗∗∗∗∗∗∗∗∗∗∗∗∗∗

Once upon a time, there was a little boy named Timmy who loved to save his pocket money. One day, Timmy's mother told him that she would give him a little extra money if he saved his money in a special bank called a "savings account". Timmy was excited to hear this and decided to start saving in his new account.

One day, Timmy's mother told him that the bank was going to give him a little bit of extra money called "interest". Timmy was confused and asked his mother what that meant. She explained that interest is like a reward for saving money, and that the bank pays him a little bit of extra money for keeping his money in the bank.

Timmy was curious and asked his mother how the bank decides how much interest to give him. His mother explained that interest rates are set by the bank, and that they can change depending on how much money people are borrowing and lending. When more people want to borrow money, the bank might raise interest rates to encourage people to save money instead of borrowing it. When fewer people want to borrow money, the bank might lower interest rates to encourage people to borrow money and spend it.

Timmy was fascinated by this and asked his mother why interest rates are important. His mother explained that interest rates can affect many things, like how much money people have to pay to borrow money for a house or a car, or how much money people can earn by saving money in the bank. She also explained that interest rates can affect the economy, because when interest rates are high, people might save more money and spend less, which can slow down the economy. On the other hand, when interest rates are low, people might borrow more money and spend more, which can help the economy grow.

Timmy was amazed to learn how interest rates can affect so many things, and he decided to keep saving his money in the bank to earn more interest. From then on, he paid close attention to how interest rates were changing and how they might affect his savings.

Relation between GDP, GNP, financial market and interest rates

Once upon a time, there were three friends named GDP, GNP, and Financial Market. They loved playing together, but sometimes they would get confused about how they were all related.

One day, they decided to play a game of tag. GDP was "it" and had to chase after GNP and Financial Market. Whenever GDP caught one of them, that person would become "it" and have to chase after the others.

As they played, they noticed that sometimes the game would go faster and sometimes it would go slower. They realized that the speed of the game depended on something called interest rates.

Interest rates were like the wind that made the game go faster or slower. Sometimes the wind would blow really hard and the game would go really fast, and sometimes the wind would stop and the game would go really slow.

But what did interest rates have to do with GDP, GNP, and Financial Market? Well, it turned out that when interest rates were low, people would borrow more money to buy things like houses, cars, and toys. This made GDP and GNP go up, because there was more buying and selling happening.

And when GDP and GNP went up, Financial Market was happy too, because more people were investing their money and making profits.

But when interest rates were high, people would borrow less money and spend less money, which made GDP and GNP go down. This made Financial Market sad because there were fewer opportunities to make profits.

So, you see, GDP, GNP, Financial Market, and interest rates were all friends who depended on each other. When one friend was happy, they were all happy. But when one friend was sad, they were all sad. And that's how they learned that they needed to work together to have a fun and successful game of tag.

****

Once upon a time, there was a village called Moneyland where people loved to trade things with each other. Some people grew food, some people made clothes, and others built houses. Everyone had different things to offer, and they would trade with each other to get what they needed.

One day, the people of Moneyland realized that they needed a way to keep track of all the trading that was going on. They decided to use little pieces of paper called "money" to represent the value of the things they were trading.

As more and more trading happened, people started to save up their money instead of spending it all right away. They would put their money in a special place called a "bank" where it would be safe and they could earn a little extra money over time.

The bank would then take the money that people saved and lend it out to other people who needed it to start businesses or buy houses. The bank would charge those people a little extra money, called "interest," for borrowing the money.

The more money people saved and lent out, the more businesses and houses could be built in Moneyland. This made the village grow bigger and stronger, which helped the people make even more money.

But sometimes, if there was too much money being saved and lent out, it could cause problems. This might happen if people started to save more money than they were spending. The businesses and houses might not sell as much, which would make them less valuable. This is why the bank would sometimes lower the interest rate to encourage people to spend more money and keep the economy growing.

So you see, the amount of money people save and spend, the number of businesses and houses being built, and the interest rate all work together to make Moneyland a successful place where people can trade and live happily ever after.

****

Once upon a time, in a world full of people and businesses, there were different ways that people could make money. Some people had jobs and earned money by working, while others started their own businesses and made money by selling things.

Now imagine that all of these people and businesses had a big piggy bank where they put all their money. This piggy bank is like the financial market, where people can save their money, borrow money, or invest money to make even more money.

As more people and businesses save and invest their money in the financial market, it starts to grow bigger and bigger. And just like the piggy bank, the financial market also earns interest, which means that the people and businesses who put their money in the market can earn even more money over time.

But the size of the financial market is also influenced by how well the country's economy is doing. When the economy is strong and growing, both the GDP and GNP increase. This means that more people are making money and businesses are doing well. As a result, more people and businesses will put their money into the financial market, making it even bigger and earning even more interest.

On the other hand, if the economy is weak and not growing, then both the GDP and GNP will decrease. This means that fewer people are making money and businesses are struggling. As a result, fewer people and businesses will put their money into the financial market, making it smaller and earning less interest.

So, you see, the financial market, GDP, GNP, and interest rates are all connected. When the economy is doing well, the financial market grows bigger and interest rates can be higher. But when the economy is not doing well, the financial market may not grow as much and interest rates can be lower.

****

Once upon a time, there was a big town called Econotown. In Econotown, there were lots of shops and factories where people worked to make things that other people wanted to buy.

One day, a man named Mr. Finance came to Econotown. Mr. Finance was very interested in the town's economy and how much money people were making. He went around to all the shops and factories and asked how much money they were making.

He learned that the more things people bought, the more money the shops and factories made. This made the town's economy grow bigger and bigger. Mr. Finance was very happy to see the town's economy doing so well.

But then, something strange happened. The people in Econotown started to borrow a lot of money from the bank to buy things they couldn't afford. They didn't realize that they would have to pay the bank back with extra money called "interest."

As more people borrowed money and couldn't pay it back, the banks started to lose money too. This made Mr. Finance worried because banks are an important part of the financial market. The financial market is like a big puzzle where all the banks and companies are connected.

Mr. Finance realized that if too many people couldn't pay back their loans, the banks might not have enough money to keep lending to people who needed it. This could slow down the town's economy and make things more difficult for everyone.

So, Mr. Finance went to the town's leaders and told them they needed to be careful about borrowing too much money and not paying it back. He also reminded them that the town's economy was connected to the financial market, which was connected to the country's GDP and GNP.

The leaders listened to Mr. Finance and made some changes to help people understand how important it was to manage their money carefully. They also worked to make sure that the financial market stayed strong so that the town's economy could keep growing.

And so, Econotown continued to prosper, with people buying things they could afford and the financial market remaining stable. Mr. Finance was happy to see the town's economy doing well, and he knew that it was important for everyone to work together to keep it that way.

Inflation

Once upon a time, there was a magical land where everything was made of candy. The people who lived there loved to buy and eat candy, and they had a lot of money to spend because they worked very hard to make it.

One day, the candy makers started to notice that the cost of the ingredients they used to make candy was getting more expensive. Sugar, chocolate, and other candy-making ingredients were getting more expensive, and they had to pay more to buy them.

Because they had to spend more money on ingredients, the candy makers had to raise the price of their candy. This meant that the people who bought the candy had to pay more money for it, too. When people have to pay more money for the same things they buy, we call it "inflation."

As time went on, the price of everything in the candy land started to go up, not just candy. Even things like toys and books got more expensive, and the people who lived there had to spend more money to buy the things they needed.

The government of the candy land tried to stop inflation by making sure that the people who worked hard to make money could still buy the things they needed without having to spend too much. They did this by making sure that there was enough money in the candy land for everyone to use, and by making sure that the interest rates were just right.

Interest rates are like a magic wand that the government uses to control the amount of money that people can borrow. If the interest rates are too high, it's harder for people to borrow money, so they can't buy as much. But if the interest rates are too low, people can borrow too much money, and that can make inflation worse.

So, the government of the candy land tried to find the perfect balance of interest rates to keep things running smoothly. And in the end, the candy makers were able to keep making delicious treats, the people who lived there could still buy what they needed, and the candy land was a happy and prosperous place.

****

Once upon a time, there was a magical land where people loved to buy things. They would buy toys, candy, and clothes, and everything they wanted. The king of the land was very kind and would give everyone a lot of money to buy things they wanted. But one day, the king noticed that the prices of everything were going up, and people were not able to buy as many things with the same amount of money.

The king became very worried and called his wise advisor to ask what was happening. The advisor explained that there was something called "inflation" happening in the land. Inflation meant that the prices of things were going up, and people were not able to buy as much with the same amount of money. The advisor told the king that there were many reasons for inflation, like when there was not enough of something that everyone wanted, like toys, candy, or clothes. The more people wanted them, the more expensive they would become.

The king realized that he needed to do something about inflation. He decided to make sure there was enough of everything in the land so that the prices would not go up too much. He asked his workers to make more toys, candy, and clothes so that everyone could have what they wanted, and the prices would not go up too much. He also made sure that people were not given too much money because if there was too much money, but not enough toys, candy, and clothes, then the prices would go up even more.

Thanks to the king's actions, the people of the land were able to buy everything they wanted without worrying too much about the prices going up too much. And they all lived happily ever after, with enough toys, candy, and clothes for everyone!

****

Once upon a time, there was a little girl named Lily who loved to go shopping with her mom. Every week, they would go to the supermarket and buy groceries, clothes, toys, and other things they needed. But one day, something strange happened. When they arrived at the supermarket, they noticed that the prices of everything had gone up. The cereal that used to cost $2 now cost $3, and the dress that Lily wanted to buy was now too expensive for her mom to afford.

Lily's mom explained to her that this was because of something called inflation. She said that inflation meant that the prices of things go up over time, and that it happens when there is too much money chasing too few goods. This means that when there is a lot of money in the economy, but not enough things to buy, the prices of those things go up because people are willing to pay more for them.

Lily was confused, so her mom used an example that she could understand. She said that it was like a birthday party where there was only one cake, but lots of people wanted a piece. If there is only one cake, but many people want a piece, the people who really want it will be willing to pay more for it. And if more people have more money to spend, they will be able to pay more for things they want, like the cake.

Lily realized that this was why the prices of things at the supermarket had gone up. There were more people who had more money to spend, but there weren't enough things to buy, so the prices went up. She also understood that this meant her mom would have to be more careful with their money, and they might not be able to buy everything they wanted all the time.

From then on, Lily learned to be more mindful of the prices of things, and to appreciate the value of money. She also learned that sometimes, it's okay to wait a little while before buying something, so that the price might go down later. And she always made sure to remind her mom to make a shopping list, so they wouldn't forget anything they needed, and would stick to their budget.

****

Once upon a time, there was a kingdom named "Happyland." Happyland had a special currency called "Happy coins." The Happy coins were used by the citizens to buy everything they needed, like food, toys, and clothes.

One day, the king of Happyland noticed that the prices of things started to rise. The king went to the market and saw that a toy that used to cost 10 Happy coins was now being sold for 15 Happy coins. The king realized that this was a problem and that something needed to be done.

The king called upon his advisors to find out what was happening. They told him that the increase in prices was due to inflation. Inflation is when the prices of things go up because the amount of money available is increasing faster than the amount of goods and services available.

The king wanted to know how they could stop inflation. The advisors told him that they could reduce the amount of money available by taking back some of the Happy coins. The king agreed and ordered his advisors to collect some of the Happy coins from the citizens.

The advisors collected some Happy coins, and soon the prices of things started to go down. The toy that used to cost 15 Happy coins was now being sold for 10 Happy coins again. The citizens were happy because they could buy things at a lower price, and the king was happy because inflation had been stopped.

From that day on, the king of Happyland made sure to keep a close eye on the number of Happy coins in circulation to prevent inflation from happening again.

Relation between GDP, GNP, financial market, interest rates and inflation

Once upon a time, there was a small village by the river. The people in the village made things like baskets, pottery, and clothing, and they would trade their goods with other villages nearby. They also had a small market where they could buy and sell things.

One day, a man named John came to the village with a lot of money. He wanted to buy many things from the villagers, but he was willing to pay a lot more than anyone else. At first, everyone was happy to sell their goods to John because he was willing to pay so much. But then something strange happened - the prices of everything in the village started going up! Suddenly, things that used to cost one gold coin now cost two, or even three.

The villagers didn't know what was going on, but a wise old woman named Mary explained it to them. She told them that when someone like John comes to town and starts buying a lot of things, it makes the prices go up. This is called inflation, and it can be bad for everyone because things become more expensive and people have to spend more money to buy the same things they used to.

Mary also explained that inflation is affected by things like how much money people have to spend, how much things cost in other villages, and how much the government is spending on things like roads and schools. These things can all impact the prices in the village and cause inflation.

Mary also explained that things like the GDP and GNP can affect inflation. If the GDP and GNP are high, it means there is a lot of money and resources in the country, which can make prices go up. And if the interest rates are high, it can make it harder for people to borrow money to buy things, which can help keep inflation under control.

So, the villagers learned that inflation is when prices go up, and it can be caused by many things like how much money people have, how much things cost in other places, and how much the government is spending. And they also learned that things like the GDP, GNP, financial market, interest rates can affect inflation.

※※※※※※※※※※※※※※※※※※※※

Sure, here's another attempt to explain the relation between GDP, GNP, financial market, interest rates, and inflation to a 4-year-old:

Imagine that you and your friends are playing a game where you trade stickers. Each of you has different kinds of stickers, and you all want to get more stickers that you like. But sometimes, some stickers become really popular, and everyone wants them. When this happens, the people who have those stickers can ask for more stickers in exchange for them. This is kind of like how prices work in real life.

Now, imagine that your friends and you are all grown-ups, and you have jobs where you make money. You can use this money to buy stickers or other things you want. This is kind of like the financial market, where people buy and sell things like stocks, bonds, and currencies using money.

Sometimes, when many people want to buy the same things, like popular stickers, the prices of those things can go up a lot. This is called inflation. When inflation happens, the money you have may not be able to buy as many things as it used to. This is kind of like if the price of your favorite stickers suddenly went up a lot, and you couldn't trade as many stickers for them anymore.

Inflation can also affect how much money you can make at your job. If prices are going up a lot, your boss may have to pay more money for the things your company needs to make the products or services it sells. This can make it harder for your company to make money, and they may not be able to pay you as much. This is kind of like how inflation can affect GDP and GNP, which are ways to measure how much money a country makes from selling things and how much its citizens earn.

To keep inflation under control, the government and the central bank may do things like changing interest rates. Interest rates are like the price of borrowing money. If the interest rates are high, it's harder and more expensive to borrow money to buy things. This can help slow down inflation. If interest rates are low, it's easier and cheaper to borrow money, and this can help boost the economy and create more jobs. So, interest rates can affect both the financial market and the overall economy, including GDP, GNP, and inflation.

****

Once upon a time, there was a town called Happyville. People in Happyville loved to buy things and play games. They used something called money to buy things and play games.

One day, the Mayor of Happyville noticed that the prices of things were going up. A candy bar that used to cost 1 dollar now cost 2 dollars! The Mayor was very worried and decided to investigate.

The Mayor found out that when there are more people in Happyville who have money to buy things and play games, the prices of things go up. This is called inflation.

The Mayor also learned that the more things people buy and sell in Happyville, the more money there is in the town. This is called Gross Domestic Product (GDP).

But sometimes, people in Happyville also buy things and play games in other towns, and they bring money back to Happyville. This is called Gross National Product (GNP).

The Mayor also found out that the people who lend money to others, like banks, can charge something called interest. This is like an extra charge for borrowing money. And when the interest rates go up, it becomes harder for people to borrow money to buy things and play games.

The Mayor realized that all of these things are connected. When there is more money in Happyville, the prices of things go up, which is inflation. But when people in Happyville buy and sell more things, it makes the town richer, which is GDP. And when people borrow money to buy things and play games, they have to pay interest rates, which can affect how much money they can borrow.

So the Mayor of Happyville decided to keep an eye on all of these things, to make sure that everyone in Happyville could still afford to buy things and play games, without the prices getting too high.

****

Once upon a time, there was a little town with a lot of people living there. These people would buy things from the stores and the stores would sell things to the people. One day, the mayor of the town noticed that the prices of things in the stores were going up.

The mayor asked the store owners why the prices were going up, and they told him that it was because the cost of making things had gone up. The cost of things like materials, energy, and transportation had all gone up.

The mayor then realized that if the prices of things keep going up, the people in the town won't be able to afford to buy as many things. This means the stores won't make as much money and might even have to close.

So the mayor decided to do something to help the stores and the people in the town. He lowered the interest rates for loans so that the stores could borrow money at a lower cost. This helped the stores to keep their prices low and sell more things to the people in the town.

By keeping prices low, more people could buy things from the stores, which helped the stores to make more money and stay open. This also helped the people in the town because they could afford to buy more things.

So you see, the interest rates and the prices of things in the stores are all connected. If the interest rates are high, the stores might have to raise their prices. And if the prices of things in the stores are too high, people might not be able to afford to buy as much, which could hurt the stores and the town's economy.

****

Once upon a time, there was a town called Econoville. The people in Econoville loved to buy things like toys, candy, and clothes. They had stores where they could buy these things. But sometimes, the stores would run out of the things people wanted to buy. And when that happened, the store owners would raise the prices to make more money.

Now, when the prices of things in Econoville went up, it was called inflation. Inflation made it harder for people to buy the things they needed, like food and clothes. That's why the leaders of Econoville had to make sure inflation didn't get too high.

The leaders of Econoville also wanted to make sure everyone had jobs so they could buy the things they needed. They measured how many people had jobs and how much money they were making by looking at the Gross Domestic Product (GDP). The GDP is like a scorecard for the town's economy. The higher the score, the better the economy is doing.

But there was one problem. Some of the people who lived in Econoville actually worked in other towns. They would earn money in those other towns and then bring it back to Econoville to buy things. So the leaders of Econoville also needed to know how much money those people were earning. That's where the Gross National Product (GNP) came in. The GNP measures how much money all the people who live in Econoville are earning, no matter where they work.

Now, when the leaders of Econoville looked at the GDP and GNP, they could tell how well the town's economy was doing. If the GDP was high but the GNP was low, it meant that people in other towns were making more money than the people in Econoville. If interest rates were high, it made it harder for people to borrow money to buy things. And if inflation was high, it meant the prices of things in Econoville were going up too fast.

So the leaders of Econoville had to keep an eye on all these things to make sure everyone could buy the things they needed and the town's economy would keep growing.

****

Once upon a time, in a faraway kingdom, there was a castle ruled by a wise king. The kingdom was very prosperous because the people worked hard and the king made sure everyone was treated fairly.

One day, a big, fire-breathing dragon came to the kingdom and started stealing all the gold coins from the people's pockets. The dragon was very greedy and kept all the coins for himself. As a result, the people had less money to buy the things they needed, and the shops had fewer customers, so they had to close down.

The king realized that the dragon was causing inflation in his kingdom. Inflation means that the prices of things get higher because there is too much money around, and people are willing to pay more for the things they need. So, the king knew that he needed to do something to stop the dragon from stealing all the gold coins and causing inflation.

The king knew that the dragon was keeping all the gold coins in a big pile inside his cave. So, the king came up with a plan to borrow some money from the financial market to build a big, strong wall around the dragon's cave. This wall would stop the dragon from coming out and stealing more coins.

To borrow money, the king went to the financial market, which is like a big store where people buy and sell money. The king promised to pay back the money he borrowed with interest, which is like a little extra money that you pay back to say thank you for borrowing the money. The interest rate was high because the king needed to borrow a lot of money to build the wall.

The king used the borrowed money to build the wall, which was very expensive, but he knew it would protect his kingdom from the dragon's greed. With the dragon safely locked up in his cave, the people were able to keep their gold coins and use them to buy the things they needed. The shops opened again, and the kingdom was prosperous once more.

In the end, the kingdom's GDP and GNP grew, which means that the kingdom's economy was strong and the people were happy. The king knew that by making smart decisions, he could keep his kingdom safe and prosperous for years to come.

Economic growth

Once upon a time, in a land far, far away, there was a kingdom ruled by a wise king. The king loved his people very much and always wanted them to be happy and prosperous.

One day, the king had an idea to make the kingdom even better. He wanted to build more houses for the people, create new shops and farms, and make new roads and bridges so that everyone could travel around easily. To do this, the king needed money, so he asked his people to help him by working hard and paying their taxes.

As the people worked hard and paid their taxes, the king had more and more money to use to make the kingdom better. He built new houses and shops, and the people had more places to live and more things to buy. He also made new roads and bridges, so everyone could travel easily and visit new places.

As more houses and shops were built, more people moved to the kingdom, and they started to make new things like clothes, toys, and food. This made the kingdom even more prosperous, and the king was very happy that his people were doing well.

This is what we call economic growth. When a kingdom or country builds more things, creates more jobs, and people have more money to spend, it grows and becomes even better. And just like the king needed his people to work hard and pay taxes to make the kingdom better, countries need their people to work hard and pay taxes to make their country grow and prosper too.

****

Once upon a time, in a land of friendly animals, there was a little rabbit named Raffy. Raffy lived with his family in a cozy burrow, and they had everything they needed to live happily. They had plenty of food to eat, a comfy bed to sleep in, and lots of friends to play with.

One day, Raffy's dad told him that they needed to build a bigger burrow because they were going to have some new friends move in soon. Raffy was excited to help, so he asked his dad where they would get the materials to build the new burrow.

His dad explained that they would need to trade with their neighbors for the materials they needed. They would trade some of their carrots for some wood, some of their lettuce for some bricks, and some of their berries for some straw.

As they started trading with their neighbors, Raffy noticed that some of their neighbors had more things than they did. Some of the squirrels had a bigger treehouse, and some of the birds had more colorful nests.

Raffy asked his dad why some of their neighbors had more things than they did, and his dad explained that it was because they had worked hard to get more things. They had found ways to make more carrots, lettuce, and berries, and they had used those extra things to trade for more wood, bricks, and straw.

Raffy was curious and asked his dad how they could make more carrots, lettuce, and berries. His dad explained that they would need to work hard to plant more seeds, water the plants, and protect them from bugs and other animals. If they did this well, they could have a bigger harvest and trade for more things.

Raffy realized that if they worked hard, they could make more things too, just like their neighbors. And that's how Raffy learned about economic growth - by working hard and making more things, they could trade for more things and build a bigger and better home for themselves and their new friends.

****

Once upon a time, there was a little village called Happyville. Everyone who lived there was very happy, but they wanted to have more things to do and more things to buy. They wanted to make their village even happier!

So, the people of Happyville decided to grow more fruits and vegetables in their gardens, make more toys and clothes, and build more houses and roads. They worked really hard and made lots of things to sell and trade with each other. As they made and traded more things, they became richer and happier.

As more and more people made and traded things, the village grew bigger and bigger. Soon, they had to build more shops and markets to sell their goods. The people also started to make bigger things like buildings and bridges. They needed more workers to help build these big things, so they started hiring people from other villages nearby.

The more people they hired and the more things they made, the richer and happier Happyville became. This is called economic growth, which means that a place is making and trading more things and becoming more prosperous. And because the people of Happyville worked together and helped each other, everyone was happy and had everything they needed.

Relation between interest rates , inflation and economic growth

Once upon a time in a magical land, there was a beautiful castle where many people lived happily. The castle had a lot of land around it, and the people who lived there grew crops, raised animals and made many things that people liked to buy.

One day, the king of the castle said to his advisor, a wise dragon, "I want our kingdom to grow bigger and stronger. How can we do that?"

The dragon thought for a moment and said, "Well, we could borrow some money from other kingdoms and use it to build more things that people will buy. This will make our kingdom bigger and stronger."

The king liked the idea, so he went to talk to the other kingdoms and got some money. They used the money to build more houses, factories, and stores. The people worked hard to make more things, and they had more money to spend. They were happy, and the kingdom was growing.

But the wise dragon warned the king, "Be careful, Your Majesty. When we borrow money, we have to pay it back with interest. If we borrow too much, we might not be able to pay it back, and we will have to spend all our money on paying back the debt."

The king listened and asked, "How do we avoid that?"

The dragon replied, "We have to make sure that we don't borrow too much money, and we have to make sure that the things we build are worth the money we borrow. If we build things that people don't need or want, they won't buy them, and we won't be able to pay back the money we borrowed."

The king understood and said, "Okay, we will be careful."

Time passed, and the kingdom continued to grow. But the dragon noticed that the prices of things were going up, and the people were not able to buy as much as they used to. This was because the prices of things were going up faster than the people's income was increasing.

The dragon explained to the king, "This is called inflation. When the prices of things go up, the value of money goes down, and people can't buy as much as they used to. This can slow down the growth of our kingdom."

The king was worried and asked, "What can we do about it?"

The dragon said, "We can raise interest rates. This means that when people borrow money, they have to pay more interest, so they will be more careful about borrowing. This can slow down the growth of our kingdom, but it can also help keep prices from going up too fast."

The king understood and said, "Okay, we will raise interest rates to keep inflation under control."

And so, the kingdom continued to grow, and the king and the dragon worked together to make sure that the kingdom was strong and prosperous for many years to come.

****

Once upon a time, there were three superheroes - Super Interest, Inflation Man, and Mighty Growth.

Super Interest was the guardian of interest rates. He controlled the rate at which people could borrow money from banks.

Inflation Man was the defender against inflation. He battled against rising prices of goods and services to keep them in check.

Mighty Growth was the protector of economic growth. He made sure that the country's economy was growing and thriving.

One day, Super Interest decided to lower interest rates to encourage people to borrow money from banks. This made Inflation Man worried because when people borrow more money, they spend more, which can lead to rising prices of goods and services. So, Inflation Man confronted Super Interest and asked him to raise the interest rates to control spending and prevent inflation.

Super Interest was hesitant at first, but he realized that Inflation Man was right. He raised the interest rates to prevent inflation, but this made Mighty Growth unhappy because when interest rates are high, people tend to save more and spend less. This can slow down economic growth.

So, Mighty Growth came up with a solution. He suggested that Super Interest keep interest rates low but increase them gradually as the economy grows. This way, people could still borrow money, but inflation could be controlled, and the economy could keep growing steadily.

And so, Super Interest, Inflation Man, and Mighty Growth learned to work together to maintain a balance between interest rates, inflation, and economic growth, and the country prospered.

****

Once upon a time, there was a beautiful underwater kingdom full of mermaids and sea creatures. The mermaids were in charge of making sure the kingdom's economy was growing, just like how you need to keep your garden growing by taking care of your plants.

The mermaids had a special treasure that they would use to buy things they needed, like food and clothes. The treasure was called "seashells," and everyone in the kingdom used them to trade with each other.

One day, a mean octopus named Inflation came to the kingdom and started stealing all the seashells from the mermaids. As a result, the mermaids had less treasure to buy things with, and the prices of everything went up. This made it harder for the mermaids to buy what they needed, and the economy started to slow down.

The mermaids knew they had to do something to stop Inflation, so they called upon their superhero friend, Interest Rate. Interest Rate had the power to control how many seashells were available in the kingdom. She decided to make it harder for Inflation to steal seashells by making it more expensive to borrow them.

This worked because Inflation realized that he would have to pay more for the seashells he borrowed, and he didn't want to spend so much. He eventually left the kingdom, and the mermaids were able to keep their seashells safe.

With Interest Rate's help, the mermaids were able to keep the economy growing by making sure that everyone had enough seashells to trade with, and that Inflation didn't come back to steal them again.

****

Once upon a time, in a magical land far, far away, there was a beautiful kingdom ruled by a majestic unicorn named Sparkle. The kingdom was filled with all sorts of creatures, from dragons to fairies, but Sparkle made sure everyone was happy and well taken care of.

One day, Sparkle noticed that the creatures in the kingdom were starting to want more things, like fancy clothes and shiny jewels. Sparkle knew that to get these things, the creatures needed to work hard and create more things to sell. This is called economic growth!

To help the creatures, Sparkle decided to offer them special unicorn coins that they could use to buy and sell things with each other. But Sparkle knew that if too many coins were made, it would make the prices of things go up and that's called inflation! So Sparkle made sure to only give out a certain amount of coins.

But sometimes, the creatures would borrow too many coins from each other and not be able to pay it back, which made Sparkle worried that the economy might not be stable. So Sparkle decided to make the interest rates higher on loans, which means the creatures would have to pay back more coins in the future.

This helped keep the economy stable and healthy, which made Sparkle very happy because everyone in the kingdom could have what they needed and wanted without things getting too expensive.

And that's how Sparkle the unicorn helped the creatures in the kingdom understand the importance of economic growth, inflation, and interest rates!

Relation between GDP, GNP, financial market, interest rates, inflation and economic growth

Once upon a time in a magical kingdom, there was a group of superheroes who always worked together to protect the kingdom from supervillains. The superheroes were called GDP, GNP, Financial Market, Interest Rates, Inflation, and Economic Growth. Each superhero had a unique power that helped keep the kingdom safe and prosperous.

GDP and GNP were like a dynamic duo. They kept track of all the goods and services that the kingdom produced and how much money it made from them. They always made sure that the kingdom was making enough money to keep everyone happy.

Financial Market had the power to control money and investments. He made sure that people in the kingdom were investing their money wisely, so they could make more money over time.

Interest Rates had the power to control how much people had to pay back when they borrowed money. Sometimes he made it cheap to borrow money, and sometimes he made it expensive.

Inflation had the power to make everything more expensive. She would sometimes make things a little more expensive so that people would buy fewer things and not run out of stuff. But she had to be careful not to make things too expensive, or else the people in the kingdom would start to get upset.

Economic Growth was the most powerful superhero of them all. He had the power to make the kingdom more prosperous, by creating new jobs, starting new businesses, and making the kingdom richer.

However, there were supervillains who tried to mess things up for the superheroes. One villain named Recession tried to make the kingdom poor by making everyone lose their jobs and businesses. Another villain named Hyperinflation tried to make everything so expensive that people couldn't afford anything.

But the superheroes always worked together to defeat the supervillains. They would use their powers to keep the kingdom prosperous, safe, and happy.

So, the moral of the story is that GDP, GNP, Financial Market, Interest Rates, Inflation, and Economic Growth are all superheroes who work together to keep the kingdom prosperous. They need to work together, or else the supervillains like Recession and Hyperinflation might take over and ruin everything.

****

Once upon a time, there was a beautiful kingdom ruled by a wise and kind princess named Lily. Princess Lily loved her kingdom and wanted it to be the best and strongest in the world. One day, she decided to build a big castle to protect her people and make them feel safe.

To build the castle, Princess Lily needed to buy lots of materials like bricks, wood, and steel from other countries. But she also needed lots of money to pay for them. She went to the royal bank and asked for a loan. The bank gave her the money she needed, but she had to pay them back with extra money called interest.

Princess Lily knew that if she didn't pay back the loan on time, the interest would grow bigger and bigger. It would be like a monster that would eat up all the money in the kingdom. So she worked very hard to make sure her kingdom was making enough money to pay back the loan and the interest.

Princess Lily learned that if her kingdom made more things, like toys and clothes, and sold them to other kingdoms, they would make more money. This is called GDP, or Gross Domestic Product. The more money her kingdom made, the stronger it would become.

But Princess Lily also knew that if too many people in her kingdom bought too many things, the prices of those things would go up. This is called inflation. And if the prices went up too much, people wouldn't be able to buy the things they needed, and the kingdom would become weak.

So Princess Lily decided to make sure the prices didn't go up too much. She raised the interest rates at the bank, so people wouldn't borrow too much money and buy too many things. This made people save their money and spend it wisely.

Thanks to Princess Lily's wise decisions, her kingdom became one of the strongest and richest kingdoms in the world. And all the people in the kingdom lived happily ever after.

****

Once upon a time, there was a group of pirates who sailed across the seas looking for treasure. They had a ship that was their home and a map that showed them where the treasure was hidden.

One day, the pirates noticed that the prices of their favorite things like rum and swords were going up. They were confused because they had the same amount of gold coins as before, but they couldn't buy as much with them.

So they went to see their friend, a wise old pirate who was known for his knowledge of economics. He explained to them that when too many people wanted to buy the same things, like the swords and rum, the prices went up. This was called inflation.

The pirates then asked him how they could get more gold coins to buy more things, like more swords and rum. The wise old pirate told them that if they found more treasure, they would have more gold coins. And if they used those gold coins to buy things from other pirates, they would help the other pirates make more money too. This was called economic growth.

But the wise old pirate warned them that if too many pirates started looking for treasure, the prices of treasure maps and ships would also go up. This was because too many pirates were trying to buy them, and there weren't enough to go around. So the prices of these things would increase, and the pirates would need to spend more gold coins to buy them. This was also related to inflation.

The wise old pirate then explained to them that sometimes, the leaders of different pirate groups would try to control the prices of things like treasure maps and ships by raising or lowering the interest rates. This was like a tax on borrowing or lending gold coins. If the interest rates were high, it would be harder for pirates to borrow gold coins, and this could slow down economic growth. But if the interest rates were low, it would be easier for pirates to borrow gold coins, and this could speed up economic growth.

And that, my little pirate friend, is how the economy works. It's all about finding treasure, buying and selling things, and making sure that too many pirates don't start looking for the same treasure at the same time.

✳✳✳✳✳✳✳✳✳✳✳✳✳✳✳✳✳✳✳✳

Once upon a time, in a land far away, there was a monster named Max. Max loved to eat candy and play with his friends. One day, Max wanted to buy a lot of candy, but he realized he didn't have enough money.

Max thought of a plan. He went to the nearby village and started working in a factory that made candy. Max worked hard, and soon the factory was making lots of candy, and Max was earning a lot of money. Max used some of the money to buy candy for himself, but he also saved some of it.

One day, Max heard that the village needed a new bridge. Max knew that if there was a new bridge, it would be easier for people to go to work and for the candy factory to sell more candy. Max wanted to help, so he used his savings to invest in building the bridge. The bridge helped the village grow and become more prosperous.

As the village grew, more and more people started to buy candy from the factory. The factory started to make even more money, and Max's savings grew even more. Max learned about the financial market, where people could invest their money to help companies grow. Max decided to invest some of his savings in the candy factory, and he earned even more money.

But one day, Max noticed that the candy factory was raising the prices of their candy. Max didn't want his friends to have to pay more for their candy, so he went to talk to the factory owner. The owner explained that the cost of making candy had gone up because the price of the ingredients had gone up. This is called inflation. Max knew that inflation was bad for the people in the village because it made everything more expensive.

To help fight inflation, Max suggested to the candy factory owner that they work to make the candy more efficiently, so they could keep the prices low. The owner agreed, and the factory became even more successful.

As the village and the candy factory grew, Max learned about the importance of economic growth, which means that everyone in the village was becoming better off because they were making more money and the prices of things weren't going up too quickly. Max knew that by investing his savings wisely, he could help the village and everyone in it become even more prosperous.

Security

Once upon a time, in a land far, far away, there was a little monster named Max. Max loved to collect shiny rocks and play with his friends in the forest. But Max was always worried about keeping his shiny rocks safe.

One day, Max's mom told him that she had found a special place to keep his shiny rocks safe. It was a big, strong box with a lock that only Max and his mom knew the combination to. Max was so happy to have a safe place for his shiny rocks!

In the same way, people also have things they want to keep safe, like their money or their house. That's where security comes in. Security means finding ways to keep things safe, so people don't have to worry about losing them.

In economics, security is also important. It means finding ways to keep the things that make our economy strong and healthy safe. Things like jobs, businesses, and the money we use to buy things.

Just like Max's shiny rocks, people want to know that their money is safe. That's why we have banks that keep our money safe and why we have laws to protect our property.

When people feel secure about their money and property, they are more likely to spend and invest in the economy, which helps it grow and become even stronger. So, security is an important part of making sure our economy stays healthy and happy, just like Max and his shiny rocks.

****

Once upon a time, there was a boy named Tim who loved to collect shiny rocks. He kept his collection in a small box under his bed. One day, Tim's mom noticed that the box was not closing properly and asked him what was inside. Tim proudly showed his mom his collection and said that he loved these rocks because they made him feel safe and happy.

His mom smiled and said, "just like your rocks, people also have things they value and want to keep safe. In economics, we call these things 'assets.' Just like you want to keep your rocks safe in your box, people want to keep their assets safe too."

Tim's mom went on to explain that in economics, security means keeping things safe, just like Tim's box of rocks. People and businesses want to keep their money and valuable things safe too, so they use different ways to do this. They might use banks to keep their money safe or buy insurance to protect their assets.

She also told Tim that governments also help keep things safe for people and businesses by making and enforcing rules that protect their property and investments. This helps people feel secure and confident about the future.

Tim smiled and said, "I get it now! Security means keeping things safe, just like my shiny rocks. I will make sure to keep my collection safe in my box."

Tim's mom smiled and said, "That's right, Tim! And just like you, people and businesses also want to keep their valuable things safe and secure."

****

Once upon a time, there was a little girl named Lily who lived in a village with her family. One day, her father, who was a farmer, told her that he was worried about something called "security."

Lily asked her father, "What is security?"

Her father explained that security means feeling safe and knowing that you have enough of what you need. He said that in economics, security means being able to have enough money to buy the things you need and want, and not having to worry about running out of money.

Lily wanted to understand more, so her father used an example that she could relate to. He told her that just like how they have to save their harvest from the farm to have enough food for the winter, people in the city have to save their money to make sure they have enough for the future.

He explained that some people work hard to save their money, while others might not have as much money as they need. This is why some people feel more secure than others.

Lily started to understand that security means being able to have what you need and not having to worry about running out. She realized that her family was lucky to have food from their farm and that they work hard to save money for the future, which makes them feel secure.

From that day on, Lily appreciated the security that her family had and promised to work hard to save her own money too, so she could feel secure in the future.

Relation between securities, interest rates, inflation and economic growth

Once upon a time, in a land filled with monsters, there was a king who wanted to make sure that all his people were safe and secure. He wanted to build a wall around his kingdom to keep out any dangerous monsters that might come to hurt his people.

But building a wall takes a lot of money, and the king didn't have enough. So, he asked the people in his kingdom if they would be willing to lend him some money to build the wall. The people were happy to help because they knew it would make their kingdom safer.

The king promised to pay the people back with extra money, called interest, on top of what they loaned him. This made the people happy because they would earn some extra money for helping the kingdom.

Now, the king also knew that sometimes the prices of things, like food and clothes, go up over time. This is called inflation. So, he made sure to borrow the money at a low-interest rate so that it wouldn't be too expensive to pay back later.

And when the wall was finally built, it made the people in the kingdom feel safe and secure. They could sleep at night knowing that the monsters outside wouldn't be able to harm them.

The king also knew that building the wall would help the kingdom's economy grow because it would make people feel more secure and confident about their future. So, he made sure to manage the interest rates and keep inflation low so that people could continue to borrow and invest in their businesses.

And that's how the king made sure that his people were safe, secure, and prosperous. The end.

****

Once upon a time, there was a big, friendly monster named Snuffy. Snuffy lived in a big, beautiful forest full of yummy fruits, colorful flowers, and lots of other animals. Snuffy loved to go out and play with his friends, but he also had a very important job. You see, Snuffy was in charge of guarding a special treasure that was hidden in the forest.

Now, this treasure was not just any treasure. It was a special kind of treasure called a "security." A security is like a special piece of paper that tells people they own a little piece of something very valuable, like a company or a building. Just like how you can own a toy or a book, people can own securities. And just like how you want to keep your toys and books safe, people want to keep their securities safe too.

Snuffy was very good at keeping the security safe. He would watch over it day and night, making sure nobody took it or damaged it. Snuffy knew how important it was for people to have their securities safe because these securities help people make money, and when people have money, they can buy things they need and want.

One day, Snuffy noticed that more and more people wanted to buy the security he was guarding. This made him very happy because it meant more people thought the security was valuable. But Snuffy also knew that when more people wanted to buy the security, the price would go up. This is because the more people want something, the more they are willing to pay for it.

But Snuffy also knew that when the price of the security goes up, it can cause some problems. For example, if the price of the security goes up too much, people may not be able to afford it anymore. And if people cannot afford it, then they will not be able to own a piece of something valuable, and that would not be good for them or for the people who own the company or building that the security represents.

Snuffy also knew that when the price of the security goes up too much, it can also cause other problems, like inflation. Inflation happens when the prices of lots of things go up, not just the price of the security. This can make it harder for people to buy the things they need and want, and it can make the economy not work as well.

So, Snuffy talked to his friends, the other monsters in the forest, and they all agreed that they needed to make sure the price of the security did not go up too much. They knew that if the price went up too much, it could hurt their friends and all the other animals in the forest. So, Snuffy and his friends worked together to make sure the price of the security stayed at a good level.

And because Snuffy and his friends did such a good job keeping the security safe and the price at a good level, more and more people wanted to invest in the forest and the animals that lived there. This helped the economy grow and made everyone in the forest happy and prosperous. The end.

****

Once upon a time, in a land far, far away, there were monsters that loved to trade things with each other. Some monsters had a lot of things, and some monsters didn't have much. They all wanted to get more things, so they traded with each other.

One day, a group of monsters realized that they could keep track of all the things they traded using a special book called a "ledger". They decided to create a big ledger that everyone could use. This was like a big library where they could all keep track of what they were trading with each other.

The monsters were happy because they could now see how much they were all trading with each other. They could also see if they were making more or less things each year. They called this "economic growth".

The monsters also realized that some monsters were better at making things than others. They called the total value of all the things the monsters in their land made each year "Gross Domestic Product" (GDP). They wanted to compare this to the total value of all the things the monsters in their land made plus the things they made in other lands. They called this "Gross National Product" (GNP).

As the monsters traded more with each other, they also started to exchange their things with other monsters in faraway lands. They created a special place called the "financial market" where they could exchange their things for other monsters' things from faraway lands.

The monsters also learned that sometimes, things could become more or less valuable depending on how much of them there were. This was called "inflation". They didn't want too much inflation because then their things wouldn't be worth as much as before. They also didn't want too little inflation because then their things would be worth too much and no one would want to trade with them.

Finally, the monsters also learned that if they wanted to borrow things from other monsters, they had to pay them back with a little extra called "interest". They set the interest rates depending on how much they wanted to borrow and how risky it was to lend to them.

In the end, the monsters learned that all of these things were connected. They needed to make things and trade with each other to have economic growth. They needed to keep track of what they were trading in a ledger. They needed to exchange their things with monsters from faraway lands in the financial market. They needed to keep inflation at a good level, and they needed to set interest rates to borrow and lend things. The monsters were happy because they learned to work together and make their land a better place.

※※※※※※※※※※※※※※※※※※※※

Once upon a time, in a faraway land, there was a kingdom ruled by dragons. The dragons were the wealthiest creatures in the kingdom because they had all the gold and treasure.

One day, the dragons decided to build a big castle to store all their gold and treasure. They hired some workers and paid them a lot of money to build the castle. This made the workers very happy and they were able to buy things they needed for their families.

The castle was finally built, and the dragons had a lot of gold stored inside. They wanted to make sure that their gold was safe and that it was worth a lot of money, so they went to the financial market.

The financial market was a place where people bought and sold things like gold, silver, and other valuable items. The dragons met some wizards who worked there, and they told the dragons that the value of their gold would go up if the economy was doing well.

The economy is like the health of the kingdom. If the kingdom is doing well, then the economy is doing well, and if the kingdom is not doing well, then the economy is not doing well. The wizards explained that the economy grows when people have jobs and are buying things, which makes businesses grow too.

The dragons realized that they had to make sure that the kingdom was doing well so that the value of their gold would go up. They started to invest in businesses and create jobs for the creatures of the kingdom.

To make sure that the kingdom was doing well, the dragons kept an eye on things like interest rates and inflation. Interest rates are like the cost of borrowing money. If interest rates are high, then it's expensive to borrow money, and if interest rates are low, then it's cheaper to borrow money. Inflation is like the cost of things going up over time. If inflation is high, then things become more expensive, and if inflation is low, then things don't become as expensive.

The dragons wanted to keep interest rates low and inflation low so that businesses could borrow money and make investments to grow. This would create more jobs, and the kingdom would be healthier, and the dragons' gold would be worth even more.

So, the dragons made sure that the kingdom was doing well, and the economy was growing. They kept an eye on things like interest rates and inflation to make sure that the kingdom stayed healthy. This helped them keep their gold safe, and it made the creatures of the kingdom happy because they had jobs and could buy things they needed.

Relation between GDP, GNP, financial market, interest rates, inflation, economic growth and securities.

Once upon a time, there was a kingdom ruled by a wise king. The king wanted to make sure that his kingdom was doing well, so he asked his helpers to gather information about how much money the kingdom was making and spending. They found out that the kingdom was making a lot of money by selling things to other kingdoms, but it was also spending a lot of money on things like castles, roads, and food for the people.

The king wanted to make sure that the kingdom was doing better and better each year, so he came up with a plan. He wanted to encourage the people in the kingdom to work harder and make more things to sell to other kingdoms. To do this, he would give them money to borrow, but they would have to pay him back with a little bit extra, called interest.

The king also wanted to make sure that the prices of things in the kingdom didn't go up too much, because that would make it hard for people to buy the things they needed. So, he kept an eye on how much things were costing and made sure that prices didn't go up too fast. This is called inflation.

The king also wanted to make sure that the people who lent him money were happy and didn't worry too much about losing their money. So, he promised to pay them back with a little extra, called a dividend. These people were called "investors" because they were investing their money in the kingdom. The place where they could buy and sell their investments was called the "financial market."

As the kingdom grew and made more money, the king noticed that the people in the kingdom were happier and had more things to buy and do. This was called economic growth. The king was happy that his plan had worked and that the kingdom was doing well!

So, you see, the king had to think about a lot of things to make sure that his kingdom was doing well. He had to think about how much money the kingdom was making and spending, how much people were borrowing and paying back, how much things were costing, and how happy the people who invested in the kingdom were. It was a lot of work, but it helped the kingdom become a happy and prosperous place for everyone to live!

****

Once upon a time, there was a big village where everyone traded different things like apples, toys, and candy. The village was so big that it had a lot of different places where people could trade things, like markets and stores.

The most important people in the village were the dragons. They had a lot of gold and treasure, and they would lend it to people who wanted to buy things but didn't have enough money. But when they lent their gold, they wanted to make sure they would get it back, so they charged a little extra called interest.

The interest was like a small fee that people had to pay to the dragons for lending them the gold. If people were able to pay back the gold with interest, they could buy more things and have a better life.

But sometimes, when people couldn't pay back the gold with interest, they would have to sell some of their things to the dragons to pay them back. This made it harder for them to buy things in the future.

The dragons also liked to make sure that the village was doing well and growing. They would check how much the village was making in total from trading things like apples, toys, and candy. This was called the Gross Domestic Product (GDP).

The dragons also wanted to know how much the village was making from trading things with other villages outside of their own. This was called the Gross National Product (GNP).

Sometimes, the dragons noticed that things were getting too expensive in the village, and it was harder for people to buy things. This was called inflation. The dragons didn't like inflation because it made it harder for people to buy things, even if they had enough gold.

To keep inflation from getting too high, the dragons would sometimes raise the interest they charged for lending their gold. This made it harder for people to borrow gold, but it also helped to keep prices from getting too high.

The dragons also wanted to make sure that the village kept growing and getting better. They knew that when people had enough gold to buy things and invest in new businesses, the village would grow and get better. This was called economic growth.

Finally, the dragons knew that lending their gold to people was risky, so they wanted to make sure that they would get their gold back even if people couldn't pay them back. So they would sometimes ask people to give them something valuable called a security.

A security was like a promise that the person would pay back the gold they borrowed from the dragons. If they couldn't pay back the gold, the dragons could sell the security to get their gold back.

And that's how the dragons helped the village grow and stay secure by using things like GDP, GNP, interest rates, inflation, economic growth, and securities.

Stock market

Once upon a time, there was a big toy store where people could buy and sell toys. People who owned the store would give some of their toys to other people to play with. These people loved the toys so much that they were willing to pay more and more for them.

Now, the people who owned the toy store realized that they could make more money by selling their toys for more than they originally paid for them. They decided to let other people buy a piece of the toy store in exchange for some of their money.

As more and more people started to buy a piece of the toy store, the price of the toys went up and down depending on how many people wanted to buy them or sell them. This is called the stock market!

Just like how the price of toys can go up and down in the toy store, the price of stocks can go up and down in the stock market. People can make money if they buy stocks when they're cheap and sell them when they're expensive. But they can also lose money if they buy stocks when they're expensive and sell them when they're cheap.

So, the stock market is like a big toy store where people can buy and sell pieces of the store itself. And just like how people buy and sell toys in the toy store, people buy and sell stocks in the stock market.

✶✶✶✶✶✶✶✶✶✶✶✶✶✶✶✶✶✶✶✶✶

Once upon a time, there was a group of people who wanted to make a lot of money. So they started a big store where they sold lots of different things, like toys and candy and clothes. They called this store the Stock Store.

People liked the Stock Store and started giving the owners money so they could buy a piece of the store. This is called buying a stock. When you buy a stock, you own a little piece of the store and get to share in the store's profits.

Some days, the Stock Store would sell lots of toys and candy and clothes, and the owners would make a lot of money. This would make the people who owned stocks very happy, because the value of their stocks would go up.

But other days, the Stock Store wouldn't sell as much, and the owners wouldn't make as much money. This would make the people who owned stocks sad, because the value of their stocks would go down.

So, when you buy a stock, you're taking a risk. But if the Stock Store does well, you might make a lot of money too!

✶✶✶✶✶✶✶✶✶✶✶✶✶✶✶✶✶✶✶✶✶

Once upon a time, there was a little girl named Lily who loved to go to the park and play on the swings. One day, she saw a man sitting on a bench with a big stack of colorful papers in his hand. Curious, she walked over to him and asked what they were. The man smiled and said, "These are called stocks, and they can help people make more money."

Lily didn't understand, so the man tried to explain it to her in a way she could understand. He said, "Imagine you have a lemonade stand, and lots of people come and buy your lemonade because it's so delicious. You could use the money you make to buy more lemons and cups and make even more lemonade. That's kind of like what stocks are - when people buy stocks, they're buying a little piece of a company that makes delicious lemonade, and if the company does well and sells lots of lemonade, the people who bought the stocks can make more money too!"

Lily thought that sounded pretty cool, so the man continued, "But just like with your lemonade stand, sometimes things don't go so well. Maybe it rains and no one wants lemonade, or maybe another lemonade stand opens up down the street and people start going there instead. That can make it hard for you to sell your lemonade and make money, and it's kind of the same with stocks - if the company doesn't do well and doesn't sell as much lemonade, the people who bought the stocks might not make as much money or might even lose money."

Lily understood a little better now, and she asked the man if she could buy some stocks too. The man smiled and said, "Well, you're a little too young to buy stocks just yet, but maybe one day when you're older and have your own lemonade stand, you can buy some stocks and make some money too!"

* *

Once upon a time, there was a magical store called the Stock Store. In this store, people could buy little pieces of magic called stocks. These stocks were like little pieces of ownership in a special kind of club called a company.

The company was like a big team of people who worked together to make something special. For example, some companies make toys, while others make clothes or even build houses. When people bought stocks, they became a little part of that team, and they could share in the magic of what the company was making.

Now, the Stock Store was a very special store because the prices of the stocks could change every day. Sometimes the price of the stocks went up, and sometimes it went down. It was like a big game, and the people who bought the stocks wanted to try and buy them when they were cheap and sell them when they were expensive.

The people who bought and sold stocks were like little wizards who tried to predict when the prices would go up and when they would go down. They were always watching the news to see what was happening in the world because that could affect the prices of the stocks.

So, if a company was doing really well and making lots of magic toys that everyone wanted to buy, the people who owned stocks in that company would be very happy because the prices of their stocks would go up. But if something happened that made people not want to buy the toys anymore, like a new toy came out that everyone liked better, the prices of the stocks might go down.

In the end, buying and selling stocks is a way for people to join in on the magic of companies and their special things. And like any game, sometimes you win, and sometimes you lose, but it's always a lot of fun to play!

※※※※※※※※※※※※※※※※※※※※

Once upon a time, there was a toy store owner named Mr. Smith. He wanted to buy lots of toys to sell at his store, but he didn't have enough money to buy all the toys he wanted. So, he asked his friends and family if they could lend him some money.

His friends and family agreed to lend him the money, but they wanted to get something in return. Mr. Smith promised to pay them back the money they lent him, plus a little extra as a thank you for their help. They all agreed to this deal.

A few months later, Mr. Smith had sold lots of toys and made a big profit. He was able to pay back all the money he had borrowed, plus the extra he had promised. His friends and family were very happy with the extra money they received, and Mr. Smith was happy because he had made a profit.

The extra money that Mr. Smith paid his friends and family is like a stock. When you buy a stock, you're basically lending money to a company to help them grow their business. In return, the company promises to pay you back, plus a little extra as a thank you.

Just like Mr. Smith's friends and family, people buy stocks because they want to make some extra money. And just like Mr. Smith's toy store, the company that issued the stocks wants to make a profit so they can grow their business even more.

That's what stocks are all about!

Bear market

Once upon a time, there was a bear named Benny.

Benny loved to go on adventures in the forest and always found lots of yummy berries to eat. But one day, Benny woke up and noticed that all the berries were gone! He looked and looked, but there were no berries to be found anywhere.

Benny was very sad and worried that he wouldn't have enough food to eat. His friend, a wise owl named Olivia, told him that sometimes in the forest, there are good times and bad times for finding food. She explained that sometimes the forest is full of berries, and sometimes it's not.

Olivia also told Benny that sometimes in the stock market, there are good times and bad times for buying and selling stocks. When it's a bad time, we call it a "bear market". In a bear market, many people are worried and don't want to buy stocks because they think the prices will go down even more.

Just like in the forest, the stock market has good times and bad times. But it's important to remember that eventually, things will get better and the market will improve. So, if you're patient and wait for the good times to come, you can still have a successful investment!

****

Once upon a time, there was a big market full of colorful balls. People would come and buy these balls when they were feeling happy and playful. But sometimes, people were not feeling so happy and didn't want to play with the balls. They would sell the balls back to the market, and the market would become sad because there were not many people buying balls.

This is kind of like the bear market. When people are not feeling good about the economy, they might sell their stocks, and the stock market becomes sad because there are not many people buying stocks. Just like how the market needs people to buy the balls to keep it happy, the stock market needs people to buy stocks to keep it happy.

But don't worry, just like how the market can have good days and bad days, the stock market can have good days too! And when the stock market is having a good day, it's like the market full of colorful balls on a sunny day - happy and lively!

****

Once upon a time, there was a group of friends who loved to collect shiny stones. They would trade their shiny stones with each other and sometimes even sell them to other people. One day, they noticed that fewer people wanted to buy their shiny stones and the prices started going down. They didn't know why this was happening, and they were sad that their shiny stones were not worth as much as before.

Their wise old grandmother noticed their sadness and asked them what was wrong. They told her about the prices of their shiny stones going down. She explained to them that just like the value of their shiny stones, the value of things in the stock market also goes up and down. When the stock market is going down, it's called a "bear market." This means that there are more sellers than buyers, and people are not as interested in buying stocks.

The kids still looked confused, so their grandmother continued to explain that just like how sometimes they don't want to trade their shiny stones because they already have a lot of them, other people might feel the same way about buying stocks. When this happens, the prices go down because there are more people selling than buying.

The kids finally understood what their grandmother was trying to say, and they were happy to learn something new. They continued to collect shiny stones, knowing that their value might go up or down, just like the value of things in the stock market.

Bull market

Once upon a time, in a land far away, there was a magical village full of happy animals. The village was full of cows, horses, sheep, pigs, and even a few unicorns. The village was known for its delicious milk, cheese, and butter, which was famous all around the world.

One day, a wise old owl visited the village and told the animals about a special kind of market called a "bull market." The animals were very curious to know more about it.

The owl explained, "In a bull market, the village is doing very well. Everyone is happy and the animals are producing a lot of milk and cheese. The demand for these products is very high, so the prices of milk, cheese, and butter go up. That means the farmers who sell these products can earn more money for their hard work."

The animals were very excited to hear this. They started working harder than ever, and soon the village was producing more milk and cheese than ever before. People from far and wide started coming to the village to buy their products. The farmers were very happy because they were making a lot of money and could buy new things for themselves and their families.

The owl continued, "In a bull market, everyone is optimistic about the future. The economy is growing, and people are investing more money in the village. This creates even more jobs and opportunities for everyone."

The animals were very grateful to the wise owl for teaching them about the bull market. They all worked hard to keep the village prosperous and happy. And the wise old owl continued to visit the village and share his wisdom with the animals.

✳✳✳✳✳✳✳✳✳✳✳✳✳✳✳✳✳✳✳✳

Once upon a time, there was a magical land where everyone loved trading. They had something called the "bull market," which was when everyone was happy and excited about buying and selling things.

In this land, there was a special kind of animal called a "bull," and it was known for being strong and powerful. When the bulls were out and about, everyone knew that the market was doing well, and they felt confident buying and selling things.

Whenever someone talked about the bull market, they would say things like, "Wow, the bulls are really strong today! That means the market is doing well!" And all the traders would feel happy and excited about making lots of trades.

So whenever you see a picture of a bull, remember that it's a sign of a strong and happy market where everyone is buying and selling lots of things.

✳✳✳✳✳✳✳✳✳✳✳✳✳✳✳✳✳✳✳✳

Once upon a time in a far-off land, there was a dragon named Bull. Bull was a very happy and content dragon. He had a lot of treasure and always had enough to eat. One day, Bull met another dragon named Bear. Bear was not happy at all. He was always grumpy and didn't have much treasure.

Bull asked Bear why he was so sad. Bear said, "I don't have much treasure, and I keep losing what I have." Bull asked, "How do you keep losing it?" Bear replied, "I don't know. One day, I have a lot, and the next day, it's all gone."

Bull said, "You need to be patient, my friend. You see, there are times when everyone's treasure goes up and down. When treasure keeps going up, it's called a bull market. And when it keeps going down, it's called a bear market."

Bear looked confused and asked Bull what he meant. Bull explained, "Think of it like a game. When more and more dragons want to buy treasure, the price goes up, and that's a bull market. But when fewer dragons want to buy, the price goes down, and that's a bear market. So if you have treasure during a bull market, you can sell it for more treasure than you paid. But during a bear market, you might have to sell it for less than you paid."

Bear looked happy and asked Bull when the bull market would come. Bull smiled and said, "You never know when a bull market will come, but it will come. Just remember to be patient and don't give up on your treasure."

And so, Bear learned to be patient and wait for the bull market. Eventually, it came, and Bear was able to sell his treasure for much more than he paid. From then on, he was a happy dragon, just like Bull.

Business cycle

Once upon a time, there was a kingdom called Econoland, and it was guarded by two dragons - Boom and Bust.

Boom was a happy dragon who loved to sing and dance. Whenever the kingdom was doing well, Boom would fly around singing and spreading joy to everyone. Bust, on the other hand, was a grumpy dragon who didn't like to do much of anything. Whenever the kingdom was struggling, Bust would stomp around, causing trouble and making everyone feel gloomy.

Econoland was a magical kingdom where people worked hard to make money and buy things they needed. But sometimes things didn't always go as planned. Sometimes people couldn't find jobs, and businesses struggled to sell their products. When this happened, Bust would rear his ugly head, and the kingdom would experience a downturn. This was called a recession.

However, things would eventually start to get better, and people would start working again. Businesses would make more sales, and the kingdom would prosper. This was when Boom would come to the rescue, and the kingdom would experience an upturn. This was called an expansion.

Boom and Bust would take turns guarding Econoland, and the kingdom would go through these cycles over and over again. This was called the business cycle.

So you see, just like how Boom and Bust take turns guarding Econoland, the economy goes through cycles of ups and downs. And that's how we have good times and bad times in the kingdom of Econoland.

****

Once upon a time, in a beautiful underwater kingdom, there lived a group of mermaids. These mermaids loved to collect pearls, which they used to make beautiful necklaces and bracelets.

But something strange happened in their kingdom. At times, the mermaids would find a lot of pearls, and they were very happy. Other times, they couldn't find any pearls at all, and they were very sad.

One day, a wise mermaid told them that their pearl-collecting was like the economy. Sometimes the economy was doing well, and everyone was happy. Other times, the economy wasn't doing so well, and everyone was sad.

The wise mermaid explained that the economy goes through different phases, just like the ocean's waves. She called it the business cycle.

During the first phase of the business cycle, called the expansion phase, everyone is very happy because the economy is growing. This is like when the mermaids find a lot of pearls. They have more pearls to make necklaces and bracelets, and they can sell them for more money.

But then the economy reaches a peak and can't keep growing forever. This is like when the mermaids can't find any more pearls. They stop making as much money, and they start feeling sad.

After the peak comes the contraction phase, when the economy starts to shrink. This is like when the mermaids have to sell their necklaces and bracelets for less money because they can't find as many pearls. Everyone starts feeling worried and nervous during this phase.

But then, just like the ocean waves, the economy starts to grow again. This is the expansion phase again, and everyone starts feeling happy once more.

The wise mermaid explained to the other mermaids that this cycle is natural and that they should always be prepared for changes in the economy. She told them that sometimes it's better to save some pearls for the future when they might not be able to find as many.

The mermaids understood the business cycle much better and learned to be smart with their pearl-collecting, just like how people need to be smart with their money during different phases of the business cycle.

****

Once upon a time, there was a magical land filled with all sorts of mystical creatures. In this land, there lived a wise old wizard who knew all about the cycles of business.

The wizard explained to the creatures that just like the seasons change from winter to spring, summer, and fall, the economy also goes through cycles. Sometimes, it's booming like a unicorn galloping through the fields, and other times it's in a slump like a sad dragon with droopy wings.

During the boom times, businesses are thriving, and everyone is happy. People are spending money like wizards throwing spells, and the mystical creatures are all doing well. But, just like the summer heat eventually fades into the cool of fall, the boom times will eventually come to an end.

When this happens, the economy enters a slump. Businesses struggle to make sales, and people start to tighten their belts like a goblin squeezing into a too-small hat. It may seem like things will never get better, but just like the winter snow always melts away, the economy will eventually pick up again.

This cycle of ups and downs is called the business cycle, and it's a natural part of the economy. The wizard explained that it's important for businesses and people to prepare for both the good times and the bad. They should save money and be careful with their spending during the booms so that they can survive the slumps.

The creatures listened carefully and promised to remember the wizard's wise advice. They knew that just like the seasons, the business cycle would keep turning and they needed to be ready for whatever came their way.

****

Once upon a time, there were five kids who loved to play different games. They had a lot of fun and sometimes, they would have a lot of toys and candy to share with each other.

One day, they found out that they had a lot of money to buy even more toys and candy. They went to the store and bought everything they wanted. They were so happy and they thought that it would never end.

But after a while, they noticed that they didn't have as much money left as before. They were sad because they couldn't buy as many toys and candy as they used to. They asked their parents for more money, but their parents said they couldn't give them more.

Soon, they realized that they had to start saving their money if they wanted to have enough for toys and candy in the future. So they started putting aside some of their money every time they received it.

Then one day, they found out that they had saved a lot of money. They went back to the store and bought even more toys and candy than they ever had before. They were happy again.

The kids learned that sometimes they had a lot of money to spend, and sometimes they had to save their money for later. This is called the business cycle, where the economy goes through different phases of growth and recession, just like how the kids had times of having a lot of money to spend and times when they had to save their money.

Fiscal Policy

Once upon a time, in a faraway land, there was a great dragon named Fiscus who ruled over the kingdom of economics. Fiscus was a wise and powerful dragon who had the ability to control the kingdom's wealth and resources. One day, the kingdom was facing a crisis. The economy was not doing well, and many people were struggling to make ends meet.

Fiscus knew that something needed to be done to help the people, so he decided to use his power to implement a new policy called Fiscal Policy. Fiscal Policy was like a magic wand that Fiscus could wave to help boost the economy.

With Fiscal Policy, Fiscus could increase government spending to create more jobs and boost the economy. He could also lower taxes to give people more money to spend, which would help stimulate the economy. Additionally, he could increase government borrowing to invest in important projects that would help grow the economy in the long run.

Thanks to Fiscus's wise use of Fiscal Policy, the kingdom's economy began to improve. More people were able to find jobs and support their families, and the kingdom became stronger and more prosperous than ever before.

And so, Fiscus the dragon proved to be a true hero for the people of the kingdom of economics, using his power to help make their lives better. The end.

✳✳✳✳✳✳✳✳✳✳✳✳✳✳✳✳✳✳✳✳

Once upon a time, there was a magical kingdom called Econoland. The king and queen of Econoland wanted to make sure that all the people in their kingdom were happy and had enough money to buy things they needed. So, they decided to come up with a plan to help the people.

The king and queen gathered all their advisors, who were very smart and knew a lot about money. One of the advisors was called the "Fiscal Advisor." The Fiscal Advisor was in charge of making sure that the kingdom had enough money to take care of everyone.

The Fiscal Advisor came up with a plan called "Fiscal Policy." Fiscal Policy is a way to help the economy grow and make sure everyone has enough money. The Fiscal Advisor explained that there were two main parts to Fiscal Policy: spending money and collecting money.

Spending money meant that the kingdom would use some of its money to build new schools, hospitals, and roads. They would also pay for things like teachers, doctors, and policemen, which helped the people of Econoland.

Collecting money meant that the kingdom would also ask the people who lived in Econoland to give them some of their money. This was called "taxes." The king and queen would use the taxes they collected to pay for the things they needed to take care of the kingdom.

The Fiscal Advisor explained that when the economy was not doing well, they would spend more money and collect less taxes. This would help people have more money to spend, which would help businesses grow and create more jobs. This is called "expansionary Fiscal Policy."

But when the economy was doing too well and there was too much money going around, they would spend less money and collect more taxes. This would help slow down the economy so it wouldn't grow too fast and create problems like inflation. This is called "contractionary Fiscal Policy."

The king and queen were very happy with the plan, and they made sure to follow the Fiscal Advisor's advice. And so, the people of Econoland lived happily ever after, with enough money to take care of their families and the kingdom growing stronger every day.

****

Once upon a time, there was a kingdom called Econoland. The kingdom was filled with happy people who lived in houses, farms, and shops. The king and queen of Econoland had a big responsibility to make sure that everyone was happy and had what they needed.

One day, the king and queen noticed that some of the people in their kingdom were not doing well. They did not have enough food or toys to play with. The king and queen realized that they needed to do something to help these people.

So, they decided to use their magic wand to create more toys and food for everyone in the kingdom. They waved their wand and magically, more toys and food appeared! The people were very happy and grateful.

However, the king and queen noticed that their magic wand had a limit. They could not keep creating toys and food forever because they did not want to run out of magic. They needed to use their magic wisely.

That's when they came up with a plan called Fiscal Policy. Fiscal Policy was like a set of rules that the king and queen could follow to make sure that they used their magic wand wisely. They decided that they would use their wand to create more toys and food only when the people really needed it, and not all the time.

They also decided that they would save some of their magic for when they needed it in the future, in case something bad happened. For example, if there was a big storm and the crops got destroyed, they could use their magic wand to create more food for the people.

The king and queen taught everyone in the kingdom about Fiscal Policy so that they could all help each other to use their resources wisely. They explained that they needed to save some of their toys and food for the future, just like the king and queen saved their magic.

And so, the people of Econoland learned to use their resources wisely, to save for the future, and to help each other when they needed it. Thanks to Fiscal Policy, everyone in the kingdom lived happily ever after.

Relation between fiscal policy, business cycle and stock market

Once upon a time, there was a town where people loved to buy and sell things. They had a big market where they could buy toys, food, clothes, and many other things. Sometimes, the people in the town had lots of money, and they would buy many things at the market. Other times, the people in the town didn't have much money, so they would only buy a few things.

One day, the mayor of the town noticed that the people were not buying as much as before. She was worried because she knew that if the people didn't buy things, the people who made the toys, food, and clothes wouldn't have any money. She also knew that if the people who made things didn't have any money, they would stop making things.

So, the mayor decided to do something about it. She decided to give the people some money to help them buy more things. She called this plan "fiscal policy." With more money in their pockets, the people in the town started buying more things again. The people who made things were happy because they could sell more things and make more money.

But then, something strange happened. After a while, the people in the town had bought so many things that they didn't need to buy anymore. They had enough toys, food, and clothes to last a long time. So, they stopped buying things again.

The mayor was worried again because she knew that if the people didn't buy things, the people who made things wouldn't have any money. She also knew that this could cause problems for the stock market, which is where people can buy and sell parts of companies.

So, the mayor decided to do something else. She decided to wait a little while before giving the people more money. She called this plan "business cycle." She knew that sometimes people buy a lot, and sometimes people don't buy much, and that this is normal. So, she waited until the people in the town wanted to buy things again.

Finally, the people in the town started buying things again, and the mayor gave them some more money to help them buy even more things. The people who made things were happy because they could sell more things and make more money, and the stock market was happy too because people were buying and selling things again.

A real world example of this is when the government gives people money to help them buy things during a recession. This can help the economy grow again and can help the stock market too. But the government also needs to be careful not to give people too much money, or it could cause inflation, which means that things become more expensive because there is too much money. So, the government needs to watch the business cycle and make sure that they give people money at the right time.

****

Once upon a time, there was a village where everyone loved to make toys. Some made dolls, some made cars, and some made trains. But one day, something happened that made it hard for them to sell their toys.

The village was hit by a storm, and many people lost their homes. This meant they had less money to buy toys, so the toy makers had a lot of toys but no one to buy them. This made the toy makers sad because they couldn't make any money and had to close their shops.

But then, the village leaders came up with an idea. They decided to give the people who lost their homes some money to buy toys. This was called fiscal policy. The idea was that if the people had more money, they would buy more toys, and the toy makers could sell their toys again.

As more people bought toys, the toy makers started making more money, and they could hire more people to help them make even more toys. This was called economic growth, and it made everyone happy because they had jobs and money to buy things they wanted.

But sometimes, the toy makers would make too many toys, and no one would buy them. This was called a recession, and it made the toy makers sad again because they couldn't sell their toys. So, the village leaders would come up with more ideas to help people buy more toys, like lowering taxes or giving them more money to spend.

This is how fiscal policy and the business cycle can affect the stock market. When the economy is doing well, more people buy stocks in companies like the toy makers, and the stock prices go up. But when the economy is doing poorly, fewer people buy stocks, and the prices go down.

In the real world, governments use fiscal policy to help their economies grow and recover from recessions. For example, during the COVID-19 pandemic, many governments gave people money to spend to keep the economy going. This helped many businesses, including toy makers, stay afloat and keep people employed.

✳✳✳✳✳✳✳✳✳✳✳✳✳✳✳✳✳✳✳✳

Once upon a time, there was a family who ran a lemonade stand. They had a big pitcher of lemonade and they would sell cups of it to people passing by. Sometimes they would sell lots of cups and sometimes they would only sell a few.

One day, the family noticed that not many people were buying their lemonade. They wondered why, and then they saw that it was very hot outside and everyone was buying ice cream instead.

The family decided to make a change. They used some of their money to buy some ice cream and started selling it alongside their lemonade. People loved the ice cream and started coming to the lemonade stand even more often than before.

The family realized that they had to change their product to match what people wanted. This is kind of like what happens with the government and the economy. Sometimes, when things are going well, the government will make a plan to keep things going well. This is called fiscal policy.

For example, if people are buying lots of things and businesses are making lots of money, the government might decide to lower taxes so people and businesses have more money to spend. This can make the economy even stronger.

But sometimes, the economy isn't doing so well. This is called a recession, and it's kind of like when the family's lemonade stand wasn't selling many cups. During a recession, the government might decide to spend more money to help businesses and people get back on their feet.

When the economy is doing well, like when the family's lemonade stand was selling lots of cups and ice cream, the stock market usually does well too. This is because when businesses are making lots of money, people want to buy their stock and own a part of the business.

So just like the family had to change their product to match what people wanted, the government can use fiscal policy to help the economy and the stock market.

****

Once upon a time, there was a big playground where all the kids loved to play. Sometimes they played really hard and the playground became crowded, and sometimes they didn't feel like playing so much and the playground was empty. This is kind of like the business cycle, which is when the economy goes through different stages of growth and activity.

Now, let's imagine that the playground has a teacher who decides to give out snacks to the kids when they're feeling tired and need a boost of energy. This teacher is like the government, and giving out snacks is like fiscal policy. When the playground is really crowded and everyone is playing hard, the teacher might give out more snacks to keep the kids going. This is like the government using fiscal policy to stimulate the economy during a recession.

But sometimes, when the playground is not very crowded and the kids are not playing much, the teacher might not give out as many snacks because the kids don't need as much energy. This is like the government using fiscal policy to slow down an overheating economy by decreasing spending and increasing taxes.

Now let's say that the playground has a snack stand where the kids can buy treats with their allowance money. This is like the stock market, where people can buy and sell pieces of companies called stocks. Sometimes, when the kids are really excited about playing and think they will win a lot of games, they might spend more money at the snack stand buying treats. This is like when people get really excited about the economy and think that companies are going to do really well, so they buy more stocks.

But other times, when the kids are not feeling as confident in their abilities, they might not want to spend as much money at the snack stand. This is like when people get worried about the economy and don't want to invest as much money in stocks, causing the stock market to go down.

So, just like how the teacher can give out snacks to help the kids when they're feeling tired, the government can use fiscal policy to help the economy during different stages of the business cycle. And just like how the kids can choose to spend their allowance money at the snack stand based on how confident they feel about playing, people can choose to invest in the stock market based on how confident they feel about the economy. It's all connected!

Law of supply and demand

Once upon a time, there was a village that had a candy shop. The candy shop owner, Mrs. Smith, had a special candy that everyone loved called "Sweetie Pops." One day, Mrs. Smith had a lot of Sweetie Pops left in her shop, but no one seemed to be buying them.

Mrs. Smith noticed that everyone in the village already had enough Sweetie Pops at home, and they didn't want to buy any more. So, she decided to lower the price of Sweetie Pops to make them more attractive to the villagers.

Suddenly, everyone in the village started rushing to buy Sweetie Pops, and the candy shop quickly ran out of stock. Mrs. Smith had to make more Sweetie Pops to meet the high demand. She also realized that she could increase the price of Sweetie Pops again because people were willing to pay more for them.

This is an example of the law of supply and demand. When there is a lot of supply and not much demand, the price will go down. But when there is high demand and less supply, the price will go up.

In the real world, this law applies to many things, such as toys, clothes, and even houses. For example, if there are too many houses for sale in a neighborhood and not enough buyers, the prices may go down. But if there are more buyers than houses for sale, the prices may go up. This is how the law of supply and demand affects prices in the real world.

****

Once upon a time, there was a magical kingdom where people loved to eat apples. There was a farmer named Jack who grew apples and sold them in the kingdom. He had a lot of apples to sell, but not many people were buying them.

One day, Jack had an idea to increase the price of his apples. He started telling everyone that his apples were the most delicious and nutritious in the entire kingdom. Suddenly, people started to think that Jack's apples were better than the other apples in the market.

Soon, many people wanted to buy Jack's apples. However, Jack had only a limited supply of apples. When people saw that Jack's apples were becoming scarce, they were willing to pay even more money to buy them. Jack saw that there was high demand for his apples and a limited supply, so he decided to raise the price of his apples even more.

Eventually, other farmers in the kingdom started to notice that people were willing to pay more for Jack's apples. They also wanted to earn more money, so they started to grow more apples. As a result, there were more apples available in the market.

With more apples available in the market, the demand for Jack's apples decreased. Jack had to lower the price of his apples to sell them. This is an example of the law of supply and demand. When there is a high demand for a product and a limited supply, the price of the product goes up. When there is a low demand for a product and a high supply, the price of the product goes down.

In the same way, if there is a lot of something, but not many people want it, the price will be low. But if there is very little of something that many people want, the price will be high. This is how the law of supply and demand works in the real world.

✶✶✶✶✶✶✶✶✶✶✶✶✶✶✶✶✶✶✶✶✶

Once upon a time, there was a candy store owner named Mr. Candy. He loved making all sorts of candies, from lollipops to chocolate bars. One day, he noticed that his store was selling out of chocolate bars really quickly. He thought to himself, "Maybe I should make more chocolate bars, so I can sell even more and make more money!"

So, Mr. Candy made more chocolate bars and put them on the shelves. However, he quickly realized that the chocolate bars weren't selling as quickly anymore. In fact, they were starting to pile up on the shelves!

Mr. Candy was confused. He had made more chocolate bars, so he thought people would buy more. But that wasn't happening. Then, his friend Mrs. Cookie came over and explained to him the law of supply and demand.

She told him, "Mr. Candy, when you had fewer chocolate bars, people wanted them more and were willing to pay more for them. But now that you have more chocolate bars, people don't want them as much and aren't willing to pay as much for them."

Mr. Candy understood. He had made too many chocolate bars, which had lowered their demand. So, he decided to make fewer chocolate bars and focus on other types of candies that people still wanted a lot.

The next week, Mr. Candy made fewer chocolate bars and put them on the shelves. They sold out really quickly, and he realized that Mrs. Cookie was right! The law of supply and demand had helped him sell more candies and make more money.

A real world example of this is the price of concert tickets. When a popular musician announces a concert, everyone wants to go and see them perform. Because there are a limited number of seats in the concert venue, the demand for tickets is high. As a result, the price of the tickets goes up. But if the musician announces another concert soon after, the supply of tickets increases, and the demand goes down. As a result, the price of the tickets might go down as well.

****

Once upon a time, there was a magical land where everyone loved to eat apples. There were many apple farmers in the land, but some were better than others at growing them.

One day, a farmer named John realized that people really loved his apples, and he only had a few left. He decided to sell them for a higher price because he knew that people would still want to buy them even though they were more expensive.

At the same time, another farmer named Mary had a lot of apples that she couldn't sell. She decided to lower the price of her apples so that people would buy more of them.

The more expensive John's apples became, the fewer people wanted to buy them. But because Mary's apples were cheaper, more people wanted to buy them.

Eventually, John realized that he wasn't selling many apples because his price was too high. He decided to lower his prices so that more people would buy them.

On the other hand, Mary's apples were selling like hotcakes, and she couldn't keep up with the demand. She decided to raise her prices a little so that she could make more money.

And that is the law of supply and demand! When something is in high demand, people are willing to pay more for it, but when there is too much of it, people are willing to pay less for it. It's like a big game of buying and selling, and it happens all the time, not just with apples, but with all kinds of things like toys, clothes, and even houses!

A real-world example of this is during the holidays when many people want to buy the latest popular toy. The stores know that people will pay a lot of money for it, so they raise the price. But after the holidays are over and people stop buying the toy, the stores lower the price so that they can get rid of the excess stock.

****

Once upon a time, there was a magical land called the Lemonade Kingdom. The kingdom was full of lemon trees, and the people of the kingdom loved to make lemonade. In the kingdom, there were two groups of people - the lemon growers and the lemonade makers.

One day, the lemon growers realized that they had a lot of lemons and decided to sell them to the lemonade makers. The lemonade makers were very happy because they needed a lot of lemons to make lemonade.

But, as the days went by, more and more lemon growers started selling their lemons, and there were too many lemons for the lemonade makers to use. This meant that the lemonade makers didn't need to buy as many lemons anymore because they had enough for a long time.

The lemon growers realized this and started to worry. They knew they needed to sell their lemons, but no one wanted to buy them anymore because there were too many. So, they decided to lower the price of their lemons to make them more attractive to buyers.

Soon, the lemonade makers saw that the price of lemons was lower and realized they could make more lemonade for the same price. So, they started buying more lemons, and the lemon growers were happy because they were able to sell their lemons again.

This is an example of the law of supply and demand. When there are a lot of lemons (supply) and not as many people want to buy them (demand), the price goes down. But when there are fewer lemons (supply) and more people want to buy them (demand), the price goes up.

In the same way, when there are many goods available and fewer people want to buy them, the price will go down. But if there are fewer goods available and many people want to buy them, the price will go up.

So, the next time you go to the store and see something is expensive, it might be because a lot of people want it, and there's not enough to go around. And if you see something is cheap, it might be because there's a lot of it available, and not as many people want it.

Relations

Once upon a time, in a magical land, there was a group of unicorns who made delicious ice cream. Everyone in the land loved their ice cream and wanted to buy it every day.

But the unicorns only had a limited supply of ice cream that they could make each day. This means they couldn't make enough ice cream for everyone who wanted it. So, what did they do?

They raised the price of their ice cream. This is because when more people want something than there is supply, the price goes up. And when the price goes up, some people decide that they don't want to buy the ice cream anymore because it's too expensive.

So, the unicorns kept raising the price of their ice cream until enough people decided that they didn't want to buy it anymore. Then, the unicorns lowered the price of their ice cream because they had too much ice cream left and they wanted to sell it before it melted.

This is the same thing that happens in the stock market. When a company makes something that lots of people want, like the unicorns' ice cream, the demand for its stock goes up. And when there is more demand for a stock than there is supply, the price goes up.

So, just like the unicorns, companies might decide to raise the price of their stock when there is more demand for it than there is supply. And when the price of the stock gets too high, some people might decide that they don't want to buy it anymore, just like with the ice cream.

That's why the stock market is connected to the law of supply and demand. And just like the unicorns and their ice cream, the stock prices will go up and down depending on how much people want to buy them and how much the companies are willing to sell them for.

A real-world example of this is when a new product comes out that people are really excited about, like a new video game console. If everyone wants to buy the console but there are only a limited number of them available, the price will go up. And if the company making the console sees that people are willing to pay a higher price, they might decide to make more consoles and sell them for a higher price than they originally planned. This can cause the price of the company's stock to go up as well because more people want to buy it.

Relation between stock market, inflation and law of supply and demand

Once upon a time, in a magical land called Marketland, there was a big marketplace where people went to buy and sell things like fruits, vegetables, and toys. One day, the price of bananas started to go up, and people were not buying them as much because they thought they were too expensive. The people who were selling the bananas noticed this and started to lower the price to attract more buyers. Eventually, the price of bananas went down, and more people started buying them again.

Just like in Marketland, the stock market also follows the law of supply and demand. When a lot of people want to buy a stock, the price goes up because there are not enough shares to go around. On the other hand, when there are too many shares available and not enough people want to buy them, the price goes down.

Inflation, which is when the price of things goes up over time, can also affect the stock market. When there is inflation, people may not want to spend as much money on stocks because they need to use their money to buy other things that are becoming more expensive. This can cause the price of stocks to go down.

For example, let's say that the price of gas in Marketland goes up because there is a shortage of oil. This causes the price of other things, like bananas and toys, to also go up because it costs more to transport them to the marketplace. This is called inflation. People may start to buy fewer toys because they need to use their money to buy more expensive gas. This could cause the price of toy company stocks to go down because there are not as many buyers.

So you see, even in a magical land like Marketland, the law of supply and demand and inflation can affect how much things cost and how much people want to buy them. And this can have an impact on the stock market too!

Relation between stock market, inflation , fiscal policy and law of supply and demand

Once upon a time, in a magical kingdom, there was a big market where everyone could buy and sell things. There were toys, clothes, food, and even dragon eggs. The price of everything in the market changed every day, depending on how many people wanted to buy it and how much there was to sell.

One day, the king of the kingdom noticed that the prices in the market were going up too much, especially for dragon eggs. He realized that too many people wanted to buy dragon eggs and there weren't enough to sell. This was called inflation.

To fix this, the king decided to use his special magic powers called "fiscal policy." He created more dragon eggs and gave them to people who needed them. This made the price of dragon eggs go down in the market because there were more to sell.

But then something else happened. People started buying more things in the market because they had more money from selling the extra dragon eggs. This increased the demand for toys, clothes, and food, which made their prices go up too. This was called a demand shock.

To fix this, the king used his magic powers again and created more toys, clothes, and food. But then the market got flooded with too many things to sell and not enough people to buy them. This made the prices go down again. This was called a supply shock.

The king realized that there was a delicate balance between how much people want to buy things (demand) and how much there is to sell (supply). He also knew that he could use his magic powers to create more things to sell (supply) or give people more money to buy things (demand), but he had to be careful not to upset the balance too much.

The king watched the market closely and made small adjustments to keep things balanced. He made sure that there were enough dragon eggs, toys, clothes, and food for everyone to buy and sell, and that the prices didn't go up or down too much. And the people in the kingdom were happy because they could always find what they needed in the market at a fair price.

In the real world, governments and central banks use fiscal policy to control inflation and supply shocks, and the stock market is affected by how well the economy is doing. When there is too much inflation or not enough supply, the stock market may go down because companies are making less money. But when the economy is doing well and people are buying and selling more things, the stock market may go up because companies are making more money.

Relation between stock market, gdp,gnp , business cycle, fiscal policy, inflation and law of supply and demand.

Once upon a time, there was a little village. In this village, there were lots of stores where people could buy things like food, toys, and clothes. These stores had owners who would sell the things that they had in their stores.

Now, the amount of things that the owners had to sell and the amount of people who wanted to buy them changed over time. Sometimes there were lots of things for sale but not many people wanted to buy them. Other times, there were not many things for sale, but lots of people wanted to buy them.

When there were lots of things for sale and not many people wanted to buy them, the owners of the stores had to lower the prices to get people interested. This is what we call "supply" being high and "demand" being low.

On the other hand, when there were not many things for sale but lots of people wanted to buy them, the owners of the stores could raise the prices because they knew people would still want to buy them. This is what we call "supply" being low and "demand" being high.

Sometimes the leaders of the village would make rules to help the owners of the stores when things were not going so well. They might make more money available for people to spend so that they would want to buy more things from the stores. Or they might cut taxes to help the owners of the stores keep more of the money they made. These rules that the leaders made are called "fiscal policy."

The amount of things for sale and the amount of people who want to buy them also affects the overall economy of the village. When lots of people are buying things, the stores are doing well and making lots of money. This makes the overall economy strong, and we call this a "good business cycle." But when people stop buying things, the stores do not make as much money, and the overall economy gets weaker. This is a "bad business cycle."

The amount of money that people have to spend and the amount that things cost also affects how much people want to buy things. When things cost more, people might not want to buy as much, and this is called "inflation."

All of these things together affect how the stock market works. The stock market is like a big store where people can buy and sell parts of different businesses. When things are going well for the businesses, more people want to buy parts of them, and the prices go up. When things are not going so well, people might not want to buy parts of the businesses, and the prices might go down.

For example, imagine there is a toy store in the village. If the store sells lots of toys and makes lots of money, the prices for the toys might go up because people want to buy them. This is good for the store, and it might mean that the stock prices for the store's parent company might go up too. But if the store is not selling many toys, the prices might go down, and the stock prices might go down too.

So, you see, lots of things affect the stock market, like how much people want to buy things, how much things cost, and how well the overall economy is doing. But it all comes down to the basic idea of "supply and demand."

****

Once upon a time, there was a big town where many people lived and did different things to make money. Some people made toys, others grew food, and some people built houses.

One day, the town leader, called the mayor, noticed that some people were buying more toys than usual. They were paying a lot of money for them because there weren't enough toys for everyone who wanted them.

The mayor realized that the toy makers could make more money if they made more toys. So, the mayor told the toy makers to make more toys, and the toy makers did just that. They hired more workers and bought more materials to make more toys.

As more toys were made, the price of toys went down because there were more toys available than there were people who wanted to buy them.

This is just like the stock market, where people buy and sell pieces of companies called stocks. When a lot of people want to buy a certain stock, the price of that stock goes up. But when there are more stocks available than people who want to buy them, the price of the stock goes down.

The mayor also knew that some people were having a hard time finding jobs in the town because not enough houses were being built. So, the mayor decided to use some money from the town's savings to pay people to build more houses. This is called fiscal policy, and it helps to create jobs and stimulate the economy.

Sometimes, the economy can grow too fast, and prices start to go up. This is called inflation. To stop inflation, the mayor can use a tool called monetary policy to raise interest rates and slow down the economy.

But sometimes, the economy can slow down too much, and people start losing their jobs. This is called a recession. The mayor can use fiscal policy again to help create jobs and get the economy going again.

So, the stock market, GDP, GNP, business cycle, fiscal policy, inflation, and the law of supply and demand are all connected. When the town is doing well and people are buying more toys, it means the economy is growing, and the stock market might be doing well too. But when there aren't enough jobs or people can't afford to buy things, it means the economy might be in a recession, and the stock market might be down.

In the real world, governments and economists use these tools and concepts to help keep the economy healthy and make sure everyone has the things they need.

Relation between stock market, gdp,gnp , business cycle, fiscal policy, , inflation and law of supply and demand

Once upon a time, there was a little boy named Timmy who loved to play with his toy car. One day, he decided to set up a little toy car store in his room. He placed all his cars on the shelves and waited for customers to come.

But Timmy noticed that sometimes there were a lot of people coming to his store and sometimes no one came at all. He didn't understand why this was happening, so he asked his mom.

His mom explained that when people had a lot of money to spend, they tended to buy more toys, including toy cars. This meant that Timmy's store would be busier and more people would come to buy his cars, and he would sell them for a higher price.

But when people didn't have as much money to spend, they would buy fewer toys, and Timmy's store would be quieter, with fewer customers coming to buy his cars. This meant that Timmy might need to lower the price of his cars to attract customers and sell his inventory.

Timmy's mom also explained that the amount of money people had to spend on toys was affected by many things, like how much they were making at their jobs (which is called GDP and GNP), whether there was a lot of money going around (which is called inflation), and how the economy was doing (which is called the business cycle). When the economy is doing well, people tend to have more money to spend on toys, and when the economy is doing poorly, they tend to have less.

Timmy's mom also told him that sometimes the government tries to help the economy do better by using something called fiscal policy. This is when they make decisions about how much money they will spend and how much they will tax people. Sometimes, if the economy is not doing well, they will decide to spend more money and lower taxes to encourage people to spend more money, including buying more toys.

Timmy's mom explained that all of these things together, how much money people have to spend, how well the economy is doing, and what the government is doing to help, can affect how busy Timmy's store is and how much money he can make.

In the real world, just like Timmy's store, the stock market can be affected by how much people are spending, the state of the economy, and the government's fiscal policy decisions. For example, when the economy is doing well and people have more money to spend, the stock market may do well, and stock prices may go up. But when the economy is not doing well, and people have less money to spend, the stock market may not do as well, and stock prices may go down.

Timmy was amazed by all of this new information and continued to run his little toy car store, always keeping in mind the law of supply and demand, and how the economy and the government's decisions could affect his business.

Relation between stock market, gdp,gnp , business cycle, fiscal policy, , inflation and law of supply and demand

Once upon a time, there was a magical land where people used special things called "money" to buy all the things they needed and wanted. In this land, there were many different shops and factories that made all sorts of things, like toys, food, and clothes.

Sometimes, there were many people who wanted to buy things, but there weren't enough things to go around. This made the things very expensive because everyone wanted them so much. This is called "inflation".

Other times, there were not many people who wanted to buy things, so the shops and factories had to lower their prices to get people to buy them. This is called "deflation".

The government in this land knew that they needed to help the shops and factories when things were too expensive or too cheap. So they made special rules called "fiscal policies" to help keep things just right.

Sometimes, the shops and factories were doing really well and making lots of things. This is called "economic growth". Other times, the shops and factories weren't doing so well and couldn't make as many things. This is called a "recession".

The government used fiscal policy to help the shops and factories during recessions by giving them extra money to make more things. This would help create more jobs and make people happy because they had more money to spend.

The government also kept an eye on how much money everyone was making and spending. This is called "gross domestic product" or "GDP". If the GDP was growing a lot, it meant that people were doing well and had lots of money to spend. This made the shops and factories very happy because they could sell more things.

Lastly, there was the "stock market". This was like a special store where people could buy and sell little pieces of the shops and factories, called "stocks". When the shops and factories were doing well and making lots of things, people wanted to buy more stocks, so the stock market went up. But when the shops and factories weren't doing so well, people didn't want to buy as many stocks, so the stock market went down.

In summary, the government made special rules to help the shops and factories make things, and they watched how much money everyone was making and spending. This helped keep the shops and factories happy, and when they were happy, people were happy, and everyone had enough money to buy the things they needed and wanted.

Macroeconomics

Once upon a time, there was a little village where lots of people lived. One day, the villagers decided to build a big playground with lots of fun equipment, like swings and slides and a big sandbox.

Now, building a playground is not easy. The villagers needed to think about lots of things, like how much it would cost to build, how many workers they would need, and how long it would take to finish. These are all things that have to do with the economy of the village.

But the villagers didn't want to just build the playground and be done with it. They wanted to make sure that the playground would be used by lots of kids for a long time. So they thought about how they could make the village a nice place to live, with good schools and parks and jobs for everyone.

This is where macroeconomics comes in. Macroeconomics is like looking at the big picture of the economy of the village, instead of just the little details of building the playground. It's about how the villagers can make sure that everyone has a good life, not just for today, but for years to come.

For example, if the villagers wanted to make sure that everyone had good jobs, they might decide to build some new factories or shops. This would create more jobs, which would mean more people would have money to spend, which would help the village's economy grow.

So you see, macroeconomics is all about looking at the big picture of how the village's economy works, and how the villagers can make sure that everyone has a good life. It's kind of like being a big boss who makes sure that everything is running smoothly, so that everyone in the village can be happy and have fun playing on the new playground.

Real world example: In real life, countries have macroeconomists who work for the government to help make decisions about things like taxes, spending, and trade. They think about things like how to create more jobs, how to make sure that everyone has access to healthcare and education, and how to make the country's economy grow.

****

Once upon a time, there was a big town with many different stores and people. Some people sold toys, some sold food, and some sold clothes. All of these people buying and selling things is called "economics."

Now, macroeconomics is like the big picture of what's happening in the whole town. Imagine you are looking at the town from high above, like a bird flying in the sky. You can see how many people are shopping, how much money they're spending, and how the town is growing and changing over time. That's what macroeconomics is all about - looking at the big picture of the economy.

For example, if there are a lot of people buying toys and clothes, that means the stores are doing well and making money. But if there aren't as many people buying things, the stores might not be doing as well. That's why sometimes people talk about things like "the economy is growing" or "the economy is slowing down" - they're looking at the big picture of what's happening in the town.

Macroeconomics is also concerned with things like jobs and money. If there aren't enough jobs in the town, people might not have enough money to buy things they need. And if there's too much money, the prices of things might go up (that's called inflation), and people might not be able to buy as much as they used to.

So, macroeconomics is like taking a step back and looking at the whole town instead of just one store or person. It helps us understand what's happening in the economy as a whole and how it's affecting everyone in the town.

****

Once upon a time, there was a big, big village where lots and lots of people lived. There were so many people that it was hard for everyone to get everything they needed. Some people had lots of food, but not enough clothes, while others had lots of toys, but not enough books.

The village leader wanted to help everyone get what they needed, so they decided to study the whole village to see what they could do. This was called macroeconomics. The village leader looked at how much everyone was earning and spending, how many things were being made, and how much everything was worth.

Based on all of this information, the village leader could make some big decisions to help everyone. For example, they could decide to build more houses so that everyone had a place to live, or to make sure that there was enough food for everyone to eat.

Macroeconomics is like being the leader of the village, because it helps us make decisions about how to make sure everyone has what they need. When we have enough houses, food, and other things, everyone can be happy and healthy.

In the real world, governments and other big organizations study the economy of their countries to make decisions about things like how much money to print or how much to tax people. These decisions can have a big impact on everyone who lives in that country. For example, if the government decides to print too much money, it can cause prices to go up and make it hard for people to afford things they need.

So, macroeconomics is like being the leader of the village, helping everyone to have what they need and making sure that everyone can be happy and healthy.

Microeconomics

Once upon a time, there was a king named Tom. He ruled over a kingdom that had many people living in it. Some people were farmers, some were craftsmen, and some were merchants.

One day, King Tom wanted to know how much his kingdom was worth. He wanted to know how much the people in his kingdom were producing and how much they were buying and selling things for. So he called in his advisors and asked them to help him.

One advisor, named Sarah, told him about microeconomics. She said that microeconomics is all about how individuals and businesses make choices about what to buy and sell, and how much to buy and sell it for. Sarah explained that microeconomics helps us understand how people and businesses make decisions based on things like prices, supply, and demand.

King Tom was interested and asked for an example. Sarah explained that if a farmer has lots of apples and not many people want them, then the price of the apples might go down because the farmer wants to sell them all. But if lots of people want the apples and there aren't many of them, then the price of the apples might go up because the farmer knows people will pay more for them.

King Tom was impressed with Sarah's explanation and asked her to help him understand more about his kingdom's economy.

So, Sarah started to collect data about what people in the kingdom were buying and selling, how much they were spending, and how much they were producing. She looked at things like the price of food, clothes, and tools. She also looked at how many people were working and how much they were being paid.

With this information, Sarah was able to help King Tom make decisions that would help the people in his kingdom. For example, she recommended that the king lower taxes on farmers to help them produce more food, which would help lower food prices for everyone.

And that's how King Tom learned about microeconomics and how it could help him make better decisions for his kingdom.

✶✶✶✶✶✶✶✶✶✶✶✶✶✶✶✶✶✶✶✶✶✶

Once upon a time in a forest, there were many animals living together. One day, a group of rabbits wanted to have a big carrot feast. However, they did not have enough carrots for everyone.

So the rabbits decided to sell some of their carrots to the other animals in the forest, such as squirrels and deer, who also loved carrots. The rabbits asked for a certain price for each carrot, and the other animals decided whether they wanted to buy them or not.

Now, the rabbits noticed that they were running out of carrots quickly and had to work harder to grow more to sell. Meanwhile, the squirrels and deer started to realize that they did not need as many carrots as they thought and started to buy fewer. This made the rabbits lower their prices so that the other animals would continue to buy from them.

This story is an example of microeconomics, which is about how individual people and businesses make decisions about what to buy, sell, and produce. In this case, the rabbits were the producers, the squirrels and deer were the consumers, and the price of the carrots was determined by the supply and demand.

In the real world, microeconomics is used to study how individuals and businesses make decisions about buying, selling, and producing goods and services. It helps us understand why some products cost more than others, why some businesses are successful, and how markets work.

Monetarism

Once upon a time, there was a magical kingdom where the King ruled over the land and made sure everyone had enough money to buy things they needed, like food and clothes.

But one day, the Fairy Godmother came to the King and said that there wasn't enough money in the kingdom to go around. The King was confused and didn't know what to do. That's when the Fairy Godmother introduced him to the concept of "monetarism".

She explained to the King that sometimes, when there isn't enough money to go around, the solution isn't to print more money. Instead, the King could control how much money was available by adjusting interest rates, just like how he could control the amount of water that flowed through the kingdom's rivers by adjusting the dams.

The King was amazed by this idea and decided to give it a try. He lowered the interest rates, which made it easier for people to borrow money and buy things. Soon, more people were spending money in the kingdom, which helped boost the economy.

A real-world example of monetarism in action is when the government or central bank adjusts interest rates to control inflation. If there is too much money circulating in the economy, prices of goods and services can rise, causing inflation. By raising interest rates, the government can reduce the amount of money in circulation, which can help control inflation. Similarly, lowering interest rates can stimulate economic growth by encouraging borrowing and spending.

****

Once upon a time, there was a wise king who ruled over his kingdom. The king knew that for his kingdom to be prosperous, he had to make sure there was enough money for everyone to use. So he called upon a group of smart people called economists to help him with this task.

One of the economists suggested an idea called "monetarism". It meant that the king should control the amount of money that was in the kingdom, just like he controlled the amount of food that was stored in the kingdom's granaries. The economist said that if there was too much money, then prices would go up and people wouldn't be able to buy as much with the same amount of money. But if there was too little money, then people would be able to buy too much, and the prices would go up too.

The king liked this idea and decided to give it a try. He made sure there was just the right amount of money in his kingdom, not too much and not too little. And the people in his kingdom were happy because they could buy what they needed with the right amount of money.

In the real world, governments and central banks use monetarism to control the amount of money in their countries. They do this by setting interest rates and buying or selling government bonds. If they think there is too much money in the country, they might raise interest rates or sell bonds. If they think there isn't enough money, they might lower interest rates or buy bonds. The goal is to keep the amount of money in the country just right, so that people can buy what they need and the economy can stay healthy.

Free market

Once upon a time, there was a king who ruled over a land with many villages. The king wanted to make sure that everyone had enough food to eat, so he decided to set prices for all the different types of food that were sold in the markets.

But one day, the king's advisor told him about a new idea called the "free market". The advisor explained that instead of setting prices, the king should let the people decide how much they were willing to pay for things, and let the sellers decide how much they wanted to sell things for. This way, the people would have more choices, and the sellers would be motivated to make good quality products at fair prices.

The king was hesitant at first, but he decided to try it out. He told the people that they could buy and sell things at whatever price they wanted, and he stopped setting prices for food in the markets.

Soon, the people began to buy and sell things in a different way. They started to trade things they had made or grown themselves, and they could decide how much they wanted to sell it for. The sellers would also make sure that their products were good quality, so that people would want to buy from them again.

Over time, the king saw that the free market was working well. The people were happier because they had more choices, and the sellers were happier because they could set their own prices and make a fair profit.

In the real world, there are many examples of free markets. For instance, when you go to a store with your family and you want to buy something, you get to choose what you want and how much you want to pay for it. And the store sets the price based on what they think people will be willing to pay. This is an example of a free market.

****

Once upon a time, in a big forest, there were many animals who lived there. Each animal had something special that they could do really well. The rabbits were really fast, the birds could fly high in the sky, and the squirrels were really good at finding nuts.

One day, they all decided to have a big party in the forest. The rabbits said they would bring their famous carrot cake, the birds promised to bring their sweet berries, and the squirrels offered to bring lots of delicious nuts.

When the day of the party arrived, all the animals gathered in the forest clearing. The rabbits showed up with their carrot cake, but they realized that they forgot to bring plates and forks. The birds came with their sweet berries, but they forgot to bring a basket to carry them in. And the squirrels brought lots of delicious nuts, but they didn't have anything to put them in.

The animals started to worry that the party wouldn't be very fun because they didn't have all the things they needed. That's when a wise old owl swooped down from a tree and said, "Why don't we trade with each other? The rabbits can trade their cake for some plates and forks, the birds can trade their berries for a basket, and the squirrels can trade their nuts for a container to carry them in. That way, everyone will have what they need for the party!"

The animals all agreed and started to trade with each other. The rabbits got plates and forks for their cake, the birds got a basket for their berries, and the squirrels got a container for their nuts. The party was a huge success, and everyone had lots of fun.

This is a free market, where everyone is free to buy and sell what they want. The animals were able to trade with each other to get what they needed, without anyone telling them what to do. Just like in the real world, people can buy and sell goods and services freely in a free market. This means that businesses can make what people want, and people can buy what they need or want at a fair price.

****

Once upon a time, there was a farmer named Jack who grew the best apples in the land. He had a lot of apples to sell but didn't know where to sell them. One day, he heard that there was a big fair in the town where people from all over the land came to buy and sell things.

So Jack decided to take his apples to the fair and sell them there. When he got there, he saw that there were many other farmers who were also selling apples, but they were not as good as his. Jack thought to himself, "I have the best apples in the land. People will definitely buy them."

As the day went on, Jack sold many apples and people loved them. They even asked him if he could sell more the next day. So Jack went back home and picked more apples to bring to the fair the next day.

The next day, Jack sold even more apples than the first day. He was so happy because he made a lot of money selling his apples. Jack realized that he could sell his apples at a higher price because they were better than the other farmers' apples. And the people were willing to pay more for his apples because they were so delicious.

This is an example of a free market. Jack was free to sell his apples at whatever price he wanted because he had something that people wanted. The people who wanted Jack's apples were free to pay whatever price they thought was fair. In a free market, buyers and sellers are free to make their own choices about what to buy and sell and at what price.

In the real world, we see this happening all the time. For example, some people are willing to pay more for organic fruits and vegetables because they believe they are healthier. And some people are willing to pay more for designer clothes because they think they look better. This is how a free market works.

****

Once upon a time in a land far away, there were a group of goblins who loved to make and sell toys. Some goblins were really good at making dolls, while others were experts in crafting toy cars and trains. One day, the goblins had an idea to make more toys and sell them to other creatures in the forest.

They set up a toy shop, but quickly realized that some toys were selling better than others. The dolls were a big hit and the goblins could hardly keep up with demand, while the toy cars and trains were not selling as well.

The goblins decided to make more dolls and fewer toy cars and trains because that's what their customers wanted. They knew that if they kept making the toys that weren't selling well, they would waste time and resources, and they wouldn't make as much money.

This is the free market at work. The goblins make toys that other creatures in the forest want to buy, and they adjust their production based on what's selling well. If something isn't selling, they stop making it and focus on what is.

In the real world, the free market works similarly. Companies make products based on what people want to buy, and they adjust their production based on how well their products are selling. This helps ensure that resources are being used efficiently and that people are getting the things they want and need.

For example, if a restaurant is selling more hamburgers than salads, they might decide to make more hamburgers and fewer salads. They want to make sure they're using their resources wisely and making the most profit they can.

Opportunity cost

Once upon a time, there was a superhero named Superkid. Superkid wanted to buy a new cape and some gadgets to help him fight crime. But he only had enough money to buy one thing.

Superkid had to think about what he wanted more: the new cape or the gadgets. He knew that if he bought the cape, he wouldn't have enough money left to buy the gadgets. And if he bought the gadgets, he wouldn't have enough money left to buy the cape.

Superkid had to make a choice. He thought about it and decided that the gadgets were more important to him than the cape. So, he bought the gadgets and didn't get the cape.

The thing that Superkid gave up, in this case, was the new cape. That was his opportunity cost. Opportunity cost is what you give up when you choose one thing over another.

In real life, we all have to make choices about how we spend our time and money. For example, if you have to choose between going to the movies or playing outside with your friends, and you choose to go to the movies, the opportunity cost is that you gave up playing outside with your friends.

Remember, when you make a choice, you always have an opportunity cost. It's important to think about what you might be giving up before you make a decision.

****

Once upon a time, there was a couple named Jack and Jill. They loved to do different things together, like going to the movies or playing video games. One day, they were trying to decide what to do with their day off. Jack wanted to go to the movies to watch an action movie, but Jill wanted to go to an amusement park to ride roller coasters.

Jack and Jill realized they could only do one of these things because they only had enough money and time for one activity. So, they had to make a choice. If they went to the movies, they would have to give up going to the amusement park, and if they went to the amusement park, they would have to give up watching the movie.

They both thought carefully about what they wanted to do and weighed the costs and benefits of each activity. They decided to go to the amusement park because they thought it would be more fun and they would make more memories there.

The opportunity cost in this situation was the movie they didn't watch. They had to give up something they wanted to do in order to do something else that they wanted to do more.

A real world example of opportunity cost could be deciding whether to buy a new toy or save the money for a family vacation. If you choose to buy the toy, the opportunity cost would be the vacation you didn't take because you spent the money on the toy. If you choose to save the money for the vacation, the opportunity cost would be the toy you didn't buy.

****

Once upon a time, there was a little boy named Timmy who loved to eat his favorite snacks - cookies and ice cream. One day, his mom gave him two cookies and a scoop of ice cream. Timmy was so excited to eat both of them at once, but he also knew he wouldn't be able to eat anything else until dinner time.

Suddenly, his dad came in and offered to take him to his favorite pizza place for dinner. Timmy was excited about eating pizza, but he also wanted to eat his cookies and ice cream. He realized that he had to make a decision: either he could eat his cookies and ice cream now and skip the pizza, or he could skip the cookies and ice cream and enjoy the pizza with his dad.

Timmy thought about it for a moment and decided to go to the pizza place with his dad. He realized that he could always have cookies and ice cream another day, but spending time with his dad and enjoying pizza was a rare opportunity. He had to make a choice and he chose what was most important to him.

In this story, Timmy's opportunity cost was the cookies and ice cream he gave up in order to have dinner at the pizza place with his dad. He had to make a choice and give up something he wanted in order to get something else he wanted more. This happens in real life too, like when someone decides to spend money on a vacation instead of buying a new phone. They have to give up the opportunity to buy a new phone in order to have a vacation, and that's their opportunity cost.

※※※※※※※※※※※※※※※※※※※※※

Once upon a time, there was a little mouse who loved cheese more than anything in the world. Every day, she would go to the store and pick out her favorite cheese. But one day, she saw a toy that she really wanted.

The mouse knew that she only had enough money to buy one thing - either the cheese or the toy. She thought about it for a long time and realized that if she bought the toy, she would have to give up the cheese. But if she bought the cheese, she wouldn't be able to get the toy.

This is an example of opportunity cost. The mouse had to make a choice between two things she wanted, and she couldn't have both. She chose to buy the toy, but that meant giving up her favorite cheese.

In the same way, when we make choices, we have to think about what we are giving up in order to get what we want. For example, if we decide to buy a new toy, we might have to give up buying ice cream. This is the idea of opportunity cost - the cost of giving up one thing in order to get something else.

So, the next time you have to make a choice between two things, remember the story of the mouse and the cheese. Think about what you really want, and what you are willing to give up to get it. That's the idea of opportunity cost.

Relation between free market, inflation, gdp, business cycle and opportunity cost

Once upon a time, there was a village where everyone loved to make and sell things like toys, clothes, and food. They also loved to buy things they wanted like candies, toys, and books.

One day, the village decided to have a big market where everyone could buy and sell things they wanted. At the market, everyone brought their things to sell and people bought what they liked.

When lots of people wanted the same thing, the sellers could raise the price because they knew people would still buy it. This is what we call "inflation".

Sometimes, people didn't have enough money to buy what they wanted, so they had to choose what they wanted most. This is called "opportunity cost".

The village also noticed that the market changed over time. Sometimes, people wanted to buy more things, and the sellers sold more. This made the village richer, and this is what we call "GDP".

Other times, not as many people wanted to buy things, so the sellers didn't sell as much. This made the village poorer, and this is what we call a "business cycle".

The village wanted to make sure that the market was always growing and people were happy, so they made sure to keep prices fair and make sure everyone had a chance to buy and sell. This is called a "free market".

In the end, the village learned that having a free market helped them grow and be happy, but they had to make sure they were always fair to each other.

Real world example: Imagine you have a lemonade stand and you want to sell your lemonade at the park. You need to decide how much to sell your lemonade for. If a lot of people want your lemonade, you can raise the price a little bit because people will still want to buy it. But if you make the price too high, people might not buy your lemonade anymore. If you sell a lot of lemonade, you can make more money and this will help your family buy more things they need. But if you don't sell a lot of lemonade, you won't make as much money, and you might have to decide to do something else with your time, like playing with your friends.

Relation between free market, inflation, gdp, business cycle and opportunity cost

Once upon a time, there was a big fair where everyone could bring their toys and sell them to other kids. This is a free market, where everyone can sell what they want and how much they want.

Now imagine that all the kids had a lot of money and they wanted to buy all the toys. This would create a situation where there's too much money chasing too few toys, which can make the prices go up. This is what we call inflation.

But sometimes, kids might not have enough money to buy all the toys. This could cause some of the toy sellers to go out of business and this would lead to fewer toys available in the fair.

When there are fewer toys to buy, some people may have to choose which toys they want to buy and which toys they can't afford. This is called opportunity cost.

As a result, the toy sellers might have to lower the prices of their toys to attract more buyers, so that they can sell more toys and stay in business. When prices of toys are lower, more kids can afford to buy them, which increases the demand for toys. This increase in demand could cause more toy sellers to start making more toys, and this could lead to more jobs and higher GDP (the total value of all the toys sold at the fair).

But sometimes, there may be too many toys and not enough buyers, which could cause some toy sellers to go out of business, and this could lead to fewer jobs and lower GDP. This is called a business cycle, which is a cycle of ups and downs in the economy.

So, we see that in a free market, the prices of toys can change depending on how much money people have and how many toys are available. This can affect inflation, GDP, business cycles, and opportunity cost.

A real-world example of this could be a farmer's market where different vendors sell their goods. When there is high demand for certain fruits or vegetables, the prices may go up, which can lead to inflation. When there are fewer buyers for certain goods, the vendors may have to lower the prices to attract more buyers, which can lead to lower prices and increased demand. This can affect the business cycle and opportunity cost for the vendors.

Relation between free market, inflation, gdp, business cycle and opportunity cost

Once upon a time, there was a village where everyone loved to trade with each other. The villagers used to make different things like bread, clothes, toys and sell them to each other in exchange for other things they wanted.

One day, the villagers noticed that the prices of some things were going up, like the price of bread was getting higher. This was called inflation.

The villagers started to worry about how they would afford the things they needed if the prices kept going up. They decided to keep track of how much money they were making and spending. This was called GDP.

After a while, they noticed that sometimes the villagers would buy lots of things, and other times they wouldn't buy much at all. This was called the business cycle.

The villagers also realized that sometimes they had to choose between buying one thing or another because they didn't have enough money to buy both. This was called opportunity cost.

But the villagers didn't want the prices to keep going up, so they decided to let everyone trade freely without any rules. This was called a free market.

They discovered that when everyone was free to trade, the prices of things would go up and down depending on how much people wanted them. Sometimes the price of bread would be high, and other times it would be low.

The villagers also realized that they had to be careful not to spend too much money on things they didn't really need. They had to think about what they wanted the most and what they were willing to give up to get it. This was called opportunity cost.

So the villagers learned that in a free market, the prices of things can go up and down, and they had to be careful with their money and think about what they really wanted. And that's how they kept their village prosperous.

Real world example: In a free market economy, the price of goods and services is determined by supply and demand. If there is a high demand for something and the supply is low, the price will go up. Conversely, if the demand is low and the supply is high, the price will go down. An example of this is the price of gasoline. If there is a shortage of gasoline due to a natural disaster or other event, the price will go up because people still need to buy it, but there isn't enough to go around. On the other hand, if there is an oversupply of gasoline, the price will go down because the gas stations want to sell it and get rid of their excess inventory.

Relation between free market, inflation, gdp, business cycle and opportunity cost

Once upon a time, there was a little girl named Lily who loved to sell lemonade. She set up a stand outside her house and sold cups of lemonade for 50 cents each. One hot summer day, a lot of people came by and wanted to buy her lemonade. Lily quickly realized she could sell her lemonade for more money and raised the price to 75 cents a cup.

At first, everyone was happy to pay the new price because they were so thirsty. But after a while, people started to realize that they could get lemonade from other kids for 50 cents a cup. They started buying less from Lily and she had to lower her price back down to 50 cents.

This is kind of like how a free market works. When Lily raised the price of her lemonade, she was taking advantage of the high demand for it. But once people found out they could get it cheaper somewhere else, they stopped buying from her. This is called competition. It keeps prices in check because if one person charges too much, people will go somewhere else.

Now imagine if all the kids on the block started selling lemonade. There would be a lot of competition and they would all have to try to make their lemonade taste better or sell it for a cheaper price to get more customers. This is kind of like how businesses in a free market economy work. They have to compete with each other to get customers and make money.

But sometimes, things happen that can affect how much money people have to spend on things like lemonade. Maybe there is a recession and people lose their jobs. Or maybe the government decides to print more money, which makes everything more expensive. When this happens, people might not be able to afford to buy as much lemonade, so Lily and the other kids might not make as much money.

This is kind of like how the business cycle works in a free market economy. Sometimes things are good and people have a lot of money to spend. Other times, things are bad and people don't have as much money to spend. It goes up and down like a rollercoaster.

Now imagine if Lily had a bunch of lemons and sugar, but she only had enough time to make one batch of lemonade. She could either use all of her lemons and sugar to make regular lemonade, or she could use some of it to make strawberry lemonade. If she makes strawberry lemonade, she might be able to sell it for more money because it's something special and different. But if no one wants to buy it, she will have wasted her lemons and sugar.

This is kind of like opportunity cost. Lily has to decide whether to make regular lemonade or strawberry lemonade. If she makes strawberry lemonade, she will have to give up the opportunity to make regular lemonade and see if she can make more money. But if no one wants to buy it, she will have lost the opportunity to make more money with regular lemonade.

In a free market economy, businesses have to make decisions like this all the time. They have to decide what products to make and how much to sell them for. They also have to be aware of things like inflation and the business cycle, which can affect how much money people have to spend. It's like a big game of strategy, where businesses try to make the most money they can while keeping their prices competitive.

Sensex

Once upon a time, in a far-off land, there were many monsters living together in a village. Each monster had a cave where they kept their treasures like toys, candies, and other things they loved. One day, the monsters decided to play a game. They called it the "Sensex Game."

In this game, each monster had to put some of their treasures into a big pot. The monster with the most treasures in the pot would win the game. But every time a monster put a treasure in the pot, its value changed. Sometimes the value would go up, and sometimes it would go down. The monsters called this the "Sensex Number."

Just like the monsters, grown-ups also play the Sensex game. Instead of putting treasures in a pot, they invest their money in the stock market. The stock market is like a giant pot where people buy and sell shares of companies. The Sensex number represents the overall value of all the companies in the stock market. It tells us whether the stock market is doing well or not.

When the Sensex number goes up, it means that the stock market is doing well, and companies are making lots of money. This is a good thing for people who invest their money in the stock market because they can make more money too. But sometimes the Sensex number goes down, and companies are not doing well. This is not good for people who invest their money in the stock market because they can lose their money.

So just like the monsters, people need to be careful when they play the Sensex game. They need to make wise decisions about when to put their money in the stock market and when to take it out. This way, they can make the most of their treasures and not lose them all in the game.

A real-world example of the Sensex is the stock market in India, where the Sensex is a widely used benchmark to track the performance of the stock market. Investors use the Sensex to make decisions about buying and selling stocks in companies listed on the Indian stock exchange.

****

Once upon a time, in a faraway kingdom, there lived a mighty dragon named Smaug. Smaug loved nothing more than to hoard treasure in his cave, and the people of the kingdom knew to stay far away from him.

One day, a brave knight decided to challenge Smaug and reclaim the treasure for the people. The knight prepared for his quest by studying the sensex, which was a magical number that represented how well the kingdom's businesses were doing.

The sensex went up when businesses were doing well and went down when they were struggling. The knight knew that if the sensex was high, the businesses in the kingdom were thriving, and he would have a better chance of finding the treasure.

So, he checked the sensex before setting out on his journey. He noticed that the sensex was very high, which meant that the businesses in the kingdom were doing well. This was a good sign because it meant that there was plenty of money to be made and that the kingdom was prospering.

The knight was able to use his knowledge of the sensex to navigate his way through the kingdom, and he was successful in his quest to defeat Smaug and retrieve the treasure. The people of the kingdom were thrilled that the knight had returned the treasure and that the businesses were doing so well, thanks to the high sensex.

In the real world, the sensex is a stock market index in India that represents the performance of the country's top companies. Just like in the story, when the sensex is high, it means that the businesses in India are doing well and that the country's economy is growing. This is good news for everyone because it means that there are more opportunities to make money and create jobs.

Arbitrage

Once upon a time in a faraway land, there were two monsters named Mike and Ike. Mike loved to collect shiny rocks, and Ike loved to collect colorful feathers. One day, Mike discovered that he could trade his shiny rocks for Ike's colorful feathers. He realized that he could use this to his advantage by trading his rocks for Ike's feathers and then trading the feathers for even more rocks with another monster who valued feathers more than rocks.

This is what we call "arbitrage." It means taking advantage of the difference in prices between two things by buying low and selling high.

In the real world, people use arbitrage to make money by buying and selling different things in different markets. For example, imagine that apples are cheaper in one market, and oranges are cheaper in another market. A person could buy apples in the cheaper market and sell them in the more expensive market, making a profit from the difference in prices.

However, arbitrage can only work if there are differences in prices in different markets, and if there are no barriers preventing people from trading between those markets. That's why many people study prices and markets to find the best opportunities for arbitrage.

****

Once upon a time, there were two fairies named Lily and Rose. They loved trading flowers and wanted to find the best price for their flowers in different parts of the fairy kingdom. One day, Lily found out that the price of flowers was higher in the east side of the kingdom than the west side.

So Lily told Rose about it, and they both decided to take advantage of this opportunity. Rose flew to the west side and bought a lot of flowers at a low price, while Lily flew to the east side and sold the flowers at a high price, making a profit.

This is called arbitrage! It's like a game of treasure hunt, where you look for the best deals and buy low to sell high. Just like Lily and Rose, people in the real world look for price differences in different markets, and buy and sell products to make a profit.

For example, if someone finds out that the price of a toy is cheaper in one store than another, they might buy it from the cheaper store and sell it at a higher price in another store or online. This helps them make some money, but it also helps to bring prices closer together, which is good for everyone.

So remember, just like fairies look for the best prices for their flowers, people in the real world look for the best prices to make some money through arbitrage!

****

Once upon a time in the forest, there was a clever fox named Felix who loved to collect berries. One day, he noticed that the berries he collected in one part of the forest were selling for a much higher price in another part of the forest. He decided to take advantage of this difference in price and buy the cheaper berries to sell them for a higher price in the other part of the forest.

Felix knew that he had to act quickly before other animals found out about the price difference. He gathered all his savings and rushed to buy as many berries as he could from the first part of the forest. He then ran all the way to the other part of the forest where he sold the berries at a higher price.

Felix had made a profit by buying low and selling high. This is called arbitrage, and it means taking advantage of the price differences in different markets.

In the real world, people use arbitrage to make money in the stock market. For example, imagine that Company A's stock is selling for $10 in one stock exchange, while in another stock exchange, the same stock is selling for $12. A trader can buy the stock for $10 in the first exchange and immediately sell it for $12 in the other exchange, making a profit of $2 per share. This is an example of arbitrage.

Portfolio

Once upon a time, there was a clever monkey named Max. Max loved collecting bananas, but he knew that he needed to be careful with them, in case something happened to his banana tree.

One day, Max came up with a great idea: he would collect bananas from different trees in the jungle, and keep them all in a special place where they would be safe. That way, if something happened to one tree, he would still have bananas from the other trees.

Max began to collect bananas from different trees, and he put them all in a special basket that he carried with him everywhere he went. He had bananas from tall trees, short trees, green trees, and brown trees. He even had some bananas that were very sweet, and some that were a little bit sour.

Max had created his own banana portfolio, which meant that he had different types of bananas from different trees. This way, he had reduced the risk of losing all his bananas if something happened to just one tree.

In the same way, grown-ups can have a portfolio of different types of investments, like stocks, bonds, and real estate. This helps to reduce the risk of losing all their money if something happens to just one type of investment.

For example, if someone only had investments in the stock market, and the stock market suddenly went down, they could lose all their money. But if they had investments in other areas as well, like real estate or bonds, they would have a better chance of keeping some of their money.

So just like Max and his banana portfolio, having a diverse portfolio of investments can be a smart way to protect your money.

****

Once upon a time, there was a little girl named Lily who loved to collect flowers. One day, she decided to make a bouquet using different types of flowers - some were big, some were small, some were colorful, and some were not.

Lily noticed that each type of flower had its own unique beauty and characteristics. She also realized that if she put all the flowers together in a certain way, the bouquet would look even more beautiful.

That's when her mother, who was a florist, explained to her that putting together a collection of different flowers in a certain way is like making a portfolio. Just like how each flower has its own unique beauty and characteristics, each investment in a portfolio has its own unique risks and returns.

By combining different investments in a portfolio, you can help reduce the risk of losing all your money if one investment doesn't do well. Instead, if one investment does poorly, the other investments in the portfolio may help make up for it.

For example, let's say Lily's mother has a flower shop and wants to invest in different companies. She decides to put some money into a company that makes flowers, another into a company that makes vases, and another into a company that sells flower arranging tools. By having a portfolio of different investments, she can help protect her money in case one of the companies doesn't do well.

Lily understood that just like how a bouquet of different flowers can be more beautiful than one type of flower, a portfolio of different investments can help protect your money and potentially make it grow even more.

Liquidity

Once upon a time, there was a garden with many beautiful flowers. Each flower had a different color, shape, and size. Some flowers were very popular, and everyone wanted to pick them. But there was one problem: some flowers were harder to pick than others.

One day, a group of fairies came to the garden and wanted to pick some flowers for a big party. They had to choose which flowers to pick based on how easy they were to reach. The flowers that were easy to pick were called "liquid" because they were like water that could flow freely. The flowers that were harder to reach were called "illiquid" because they were like ice that couldn't move easily.

The fairies realized that they needed to balance their choices to make sure they had enough liquid flowers for the party. If they only picked the liquid flowers, the illiquid flowers would be left behind and might wilt away. But if they picked too many illiquid flowers, they might not have enough time to get them all and miss the party. So they created a portfolio of flowers with a mix of liquid and illiquid flowers that they could easily pick in time for the party.

In the real world, liquidity is important for businesses and investors who need to balance their choices between assets that are easy to sell, like cash or stocks, and assets that are harder to sell, like real estate or collectibles. For example, a business might keep some cash on hand to pay its bills, but also invest some of its money in stocks or bonds that could earn more money over time. By creating a portfolio of liquid and illiquid assets, they can balance their needs for money now and money later.

****

Once upon a time, in a land of dragons, there was a dragon named Drako. Drako loved to collect gold coins and shiny jewels. One day, he heard that there was a treasure chest full of gold coins and jewels hidden in a faraway cave. He immediately set out on a journey to find the treasure.

On the way, Drako met another dragon named Sparky. Sparky was in a hurry to buy some tasty dragon fruits, but he didn't have any gold coins with him. Drako offered to sell some of his coins to Sparky, but Sparky only had some smaller jewels to trade.

Drako wanted to help Sparky, but he also didn't want to give away all of his valuable coins. So, he decided to sell Sparky only a few coins, but he also asked for a trade of Sparky's jewels. This way, Drako could keep some of his coins and also get some smaller jewels that he could use for buying things in the future.

This is similar to what we call "liquidity" in the grown-up world. Liquidity is like having enough coins or jewels that are easy to trade for things you want to buy. Just like Drako had some coins and also got some jewels in return that he could use in the future.

A real world example of liquidity is having enough money in a savings account or a checking account that you can easily withdraw or transfer to buy things you need. Just like how Drako had coins and jewels that he could use to buy things he wanted.

****

Once upon a time, there was a little fairy named Lily who had a jar full of magical fairy dust. She loved her fairy dust so much, but sometimes she needed to use it to buy things she needed. One day, she wanted to buy a new dress for her best friend's birthday party, but she didn't have enough fairy dust in her jar.

Luckily, Lily knew about a place where she could go to trade her fairy dust for more fairy dust or other things she needed. This place was called the Fairy Market, and it was filled with other fairies selling their own magical items.

When she got to the Fairy Market, she saw many fairies buying and selling their things. Some fairies were selling flower petals, some were selling fruits, and some were selling shiny stones. Lily asked around and found out that she could trade her jar of fairy dust for some shiny stones.

But Lily was very smart, and she knew that she might need to use her fairy dust again soon, so she didn't want to trade all of it for shiny stones. Instead, she decided to trade only some of it for the shiny stones, so she could keep some fairy dust left in her jar.

This is what we call liquidity, Lily knew that she needed to keep some of her fairy dust easily accessible so that she could use it whenever she needed to buy something else. She had to make sure that she didn't trade all of her fairy dust for other things that she couldn't easily use later on.

Just like Lily, people and businesses also need to keep some of their money or assets easily accessible, in case they need it quickly. This is why banks keep some money in their vaults, and people keep some money in their wallets or savings accounts. This is what we call liquidity.

A real-world example of liquidity is when a company keeps some cash on hand, or in a savings account, so they can pay for any unexpected expenses or emergencies that might come up.

****

Once upon a time, there was a dog named Max who loved to play with his toys. Max had a collection of toys such as a ball, a rope, and a squeaky toy. Max's friend, Lily, also had some toys, including a chew toy and a frisbee.

One day, Max's owner went to the store and bought Max a new toy, a shiny red ball. Max was very happy to have a new toy, but he realized he had too many toys now and didn't have enough space to keep them all. He started to think about which toys he wanted to keep and which ones he could give to Lily.

Max knew that some toys were more popular than others, and if he gave away his favorite toy, he might regret it later. He decided to keep his ball and his rope, and give Lily his squeaky toy. Max thought that Lily might like it more than he did, and he could always borrow it from her later.

Max had made a smart decision. He had used his knowledge about which toys were more valuable and which ones were less valuable to make a good choice. This is similar to what people do when they have money to invest in the stock market. They have to decide which stocks to buy and which ones to sell, based on how much they think they are worth.

Sometimes, people need to sell their stocks quickly to get money for something they need, like paying for a car repair. The ability to sell stocks quickly is called liquidity. Just like Max had to decide which toys to keep and which ones to give away, people who invest in the stock market need to decide which stocks to keep for the long term and which ones to sell quickly if they need to get their money back.

A real-world example of liquidity is when someone needs to sell their car quickly because they need money for an emergency. If their car is very popular and many people want to buy it, it is said to be a "liquid" asset because it is easy to sell quickly. But if their car is old and no one wants to buy it, it is said to be "illiquid" because it would be hard to sell quickly. The same goes for stocks in the stock market - some are more liquid than others, depending on how many people want to buy and sell them.

****

Once upon a time, there was a powerful king who owned a big castle filled with many treasures, such as gold, silver, and jewels. One day, the king needed some money to pay for his army, but he didn't want to sell any of his precious treasures because they were too valuable to him.

So the king decided to borrow some money from his friends, who were also kings and wealthy rulers. He promised to pay them back with interest in a year's time. The friends agreed, but they also wanted to make sure that the king could pay them back. They asked him to show them that he had enough money to do so.

The king realized that he needed to have some "liquidity" or cash on hand to prove to his friends that he could repay them. So he decided to sell some of his less valuable items, such as old weapons and armor, to get the cash he needed. This was a good solution for the king because he still had his most precious treasures, and he could also show his friends that he had enough money to pay them back.

In the real world, liquidity is important for businesses and individuals because it refers to how easily they can convert their assets into cash without losing value. For example, if a company needs to pay its employees or suppliers, it must have enough cash on hand to do so. If the company's assets are not very liquid, it may need to sell them at a lower price than their actual value, which would result in a loss. Therefore, it is important for companies to manage their liquidity carefully to ensure that they have enough cash to meet their obligations without having to sell their assets at a loss.

****

Once upon a time, there was a beautiful garden with many different kinds of plants growing in it. Each plant was unique and had different needs to grow healthy and strong. Some plants needed lots of water, while others needed more sunlight, and some needed special soil to thrive.

Now imagine you are the owner of this garden, and you have to make sure all the plants get what they need to grow well. But what if one day, you need to buy some important things for your family and you don't have enough money? You might think about selling some of the plants to get the money you need.

But you must be careful when choosing which plants to sell. You don't want to sell the plants that are your favorites or that will take a long time to grow again. Instead, you might choose to sell some of the plants that don't need as much care or are more common, like the daisies or the marigolds. These plants are more "liquid," meaning they can be easily sold for money without losing too much value.

In the same way, companies and governments also need to have "liquid" assets to be able to pay for things they need. They can't just sell everything they have, because some things might be too important or take too long to replace. Instead, they might choose to keep some of their money in cash or other easy-to-sell investments like stocks or bonds. These are considered "liquid" assets because they can be quickly converted into cash without losing too much value.

Real-world example: Imagine a company that needs to pay its employees every month. To make sure they always have enough money to pay their workers, they might keep some of their cash in a savings account or invest in stocks that can be easily sold if needed. This way, they have "liquid" assets that they can use to pay their bills, even if they don't have enough money coming in from sales or other sources.

****

Once upon a time, there was a magical land called Fairyland. The fairies in this land loved to collect shiny objects, like crystals, gems, and even gold coins. They kept their treasures safe in little chests in their homes. One day, a fairy named Lily realized she needed to buy a new dress for a royal ball, but she didn't have enough gold coins to buy it.

So, Lily decided to sell one of her crystal collections to get some gold coins. But, she found out that nobody wanted to buy her crystals. She felt sad and frustrated because she needed the coins urgently. Then, her friend Ruby told her about the importance of liquidity. She explained that liquidity means how quickly and easily you can turn something into money.

Lily realized that her crystals were not very liquid because not many people wanted to buy them, but gold coins were very liquid because everyone in Fairyland accepted them as money. So, she decided to sell some of her gold coins instead of the crystals, and she was able to get the coins she needed to buy her new dress for the ball.

In the real world, people often talk about liquidity when they are talking about investments. For example, stocks in big, well-known companies are usually very liquid because many people want to buy and sell them. But, shares in smaller companies that are not as well-known might not be as liquid because there are not as many people interested in buying them. So, if you need to sell your shares quickly, it might be harder to find someone who wants to buy them.

****

Once upon a time, there was a great and powerful king who ruled over a prosperous kingdom. The king had many treasures, including a large amount of gold and silver coins, precious gems, and valuable works of art.

One day, the king learned about the concept of liquidity, which refers to how easily something can be turned into cash. The king realized that while his treasures were valuable, they were not very liquid because they were not easily convertible into cash.

To increase his liquidity, the king decided to invest some of his wealth into businesses that were doing well in his kingdom. By owning a portion of these successful businesses, the king could earn profits and receive regular payments in the form of dividends, which would increase his cash flow and improve his liquidity.

For example, the king invested in a successful blacksmith who made weapons for his army. He also invested in a popular bakery that made delicious pastries for his kingdom. By investing in these businesses, the king not only helped them grow but also ensured a steady stream of income for himself.

In the real world, people can also invest in businesses by buying stocks, which represent ownership in a company. By investing in stocks, people can potentially earn profits and receive dividends, which can improve their liquidity. However, it's important to remember that investing always comes with risks and it's important to do research and seek advice before making any investment decisions.

Equity

Once upon a time, there were three little animals: a rabbit, a fox, and a deer. One day, they found a basket of juicy, ripe berries in the forest.

The rabbit said, "I think we should divide the berries equally between us. We are all friends and we should share them fairly."

The fox disagreed and said, "I don't think that's fair. I am faster than both of you and I caught the basket first. I should get more berries."

The deer said, "I understand what you're saying, Fox, but we should also think about who needs the berries the most. I have a big family to feed and could really use more berries."

They couldn't agree on how to divide the berries, so they decided to ask the wise owl for advice. The owl listened to their arguments and suggested that they distribute the berries based on their needs, not just their wants or abilities.

The rabbit got the fewest berries because he had enough to eat for the day. The fox got a little more because he needed some energy to run around and hunt. The deer got the most because she had to feed her family and needed the most sustenance.

This, my dear friend, is what equity means. It's about distributing resources fairly based on who needs them the most, rather than just dividing them equally or giving more to those who are more capable.

In the real world, governments and organizations try to create equity by providing resources to those who need them the most. For example, they may provide free meals to low-income families or scholarships to students who cannot afford college.

✶✶✶✶✶✶✶✶✶✶✶✶✶✶✶✶✶✶✶✶✶✶

Once upon a time, there was a farm where all the animals lived together. One day, the farmer came and asked the animals if they wanted to share the fruits of their labor equally. All the animals agreed except for the cows, who thought that they should get more because they gave the most milk.

The farmer explained to the cows that just because they gave more milk, it didn't mean they deserved more food than the other animals. He said that it was important to be fair and to treat everyone equally. This is what equity means - making sure that everyone gets what they deserve, no matter how much they give or how much they have.

In the end, the cows agreed and they all shared the food equally. They realized that it felt good to be fair and to help each other out.

In the real world, equity is important for ensuring that everyone has access to basic needs like healthcare, education, and food. For example, some children may have more resources than others, but it's important to make sure that every child has the opportunity to succeed and reach their full potential, no matter their background. By creating a more equitable society, we can help everyone thrive and live their best life.

Investing

Once upon a time, in a magical kingdom, there were some fairies who loved to collect shiny things like gold and gems. One day, they decided to invest their treasures in a special tree that was known to grow more treasures over time.

The fairies understood that by investing their treasures in the tree, they were giving them away for a while, but they also knew that the tree would grow more treasures that they could enjoy later on.

As the days went by, the tree grew bigger and bigger, and it started to produce more and more treasures. The fairies were very happy because they had made a good investment.

In the real world, people also invest their money to make it grow over time. They might invest in stocks, bonds, or real estate, and by doing so, they hope to earn more money in the future. Just like the fairies, they have to be patient and wait for their investments to grow, but in the end, it can be worth it.

Trading

Once upon a time, in a magical forest, there lived a group of fairies who loved to collect and trade different kinds of berries. Each fairy had their own collection of berries, but they also loved to trade with each other to get new and interesting types of berries.

One day, a group of new fairies came to the forest and they brought with them some rare and special berries that the other fairies had never seen before. The other fairies were very excited and wanted to trade for these special berries.

The new fairies asked for some of the other fairies' berries in exchange, but they wanted more than what the berries were worth. They thought they could get more berries than what they were giving away. This is called trading.

Some fairies were happy to make the trade, but others were not. They thought it wasn't fair to give away so many berries for just a few special ones. They wanted to wait until the new fairies were willing to trade for a fairer price. This is called investing, which means waiting to make a trade until you think the price is right.

After a while, the new fairies realized that they weren't getting as many berries as they wanted because the other fairies thought they were asking for too much. So, they lowered the price of their special berries, and more fairies were willing to trade with them.

In the end, all the fairies were happy because they were able to get new and interesting berries through trading and investing. And they all learned the importance of making fair trades and waiting for the right price.

Just like fairies, people in the real world also trade and invest in things like stocks and commodities. Some people like to make quick trades, while others prefer to wait and invest for the long term. It's important to make smart decisions and be patient when investing and trading.

****

Once upon a time, in a magical world far, far away, there was a place called the Trading Kingdom. This kingdom was filled with all sorts of creatures like unicorns, dragons, and fairies.

The fairies loved to trade their special fairy dust for other things they needed, like food and clothes. They would meet at a special place called the Trading Tree, where they would exchange their fairy dust with other fairies who had things they wanted.

Sometimes, a fairy would have a lot of fairy dust and would want to trade it for something really special, like a magical crystal. But the fairy who had the crystal might not want any fairy dust at all - maybe they wanted a shiny unicorn horn instead!

So, the fairies learned to trade with each other, making deals that would make both of them happy. They would negotiate and haggle, trying to get the best deal they could.

In the real world, trading is a lot like what the fairies did. People trade things they have for things they want. Sometimes they buy things they need, like food and clothes, and sometimes they buy things they want, like toys and games.

When people trade stocks or other investments, they're doing something similar to what the fairies did at the Trading Tree. They're exchanging one thing (like money) for something else (like a share of a company).

And just like the fairies, people who trade in the real world try to make good deals that will make them happy. They watch the prices of things they want to buy, and they try to buy when the price is low. And they watch the prices of things they own, and they try to sell when the price is high.

A real-world example of trading might be when someone buys shares of a company that they think will do well in the future. They might hold on to those shares for a while and then sell them later when the price goes up, hopefully making a profit.

Trading in stock market

Once upon a time, in a magical kingdom, there was a fairy named Lily who loved to collect magical seeds that grew into beautiful flowers. One day, her friend, a fairy named Rose, came to her and said, "Lily, I have a magical seed that will grow into a rare flower. But I need some help in growing it."

Lily asked, "What kind of help do you need, Rose?"

Rose replied, "I need some money to buy special soil and fertilizer for this seed to grow into a beautiful flower."

Lily thought for a moment and said, "I can give you the money you need, but I want something in return."

Rose asked, "What do you want?"

Lily said, "I want a part of the rare flower when it grows. That way, I can add it to my flower collection."

Rose thought it was a good deal and agreed. But then, she had an idea. She said, "Lily, instead of giving you a part of the flower, how about I give you some money back along with the flower? That way, we can both benefit."

Lily was curious and asked, "How can we both benefit?"

Rose explained, "We can sell the flower in the market for a higher price than what we invested in it. That way, we make a profit."

Lily was excited and asked, "How do we sell the flower in the market?"

Rose replied, "We can take the flower to the market and find someone who wants to buy it. That's called trading."

Lily understood and said, "That sounds like fun! Let's do it."

So, they invested their money and grew the rare flower. When the flower bloomed, it was indeed beautiful, and they took it to the market to find a buyer. Luckily, they found a buyer who was willing to pay a high price for the rare flower. They sold the flower and made a profit, and Lily was happy to add it to her flower collection.

Just like Lily and Rose, people can invest their money in stocks, which are like seeds that grow into companies. They can then sell their stocks in the market when the company is doing well, and they can make a profit just like Lily and Rose did. This is called trading in the stock market.

Difference between investing and trading in stock market.

Once upon a time in the land of Fairies, there lived two friends named Investing and Trading. Investing loved to collect shiny stones and keep them safe in her magical pouch. Trading, on the other hand, loved to exchange shiny stones with others in the market to earn more stones.

One day, they both went to the Stone Market where Investing saw a beautiful blue stone. She wanted to keep it in her pouch and watch it grow bigger and shinier over time. But Trading thought that the blue stone was valuable and he wanted to buy it to sell it for more stones in the future.

Investing and Trading had different goals. Investing wanted to hold on to the stone for a long time and let it grow, while Trading wanted to buy and sell quickly to make a profit. This is the difference between investing and trading in the stock market.

In the real world, people who invest in the stock market buy stocks of companies they believe will grow over time, and hold on to them for years. They might earn money from the company's profits or by selling the stock for a higher price than they bought it for. This is similar to how Investing likes to keep her stones and watch them grow.

On the other hand, people who trade in the stock market buy and sell stocks quickly to make a profit in a short amount of time. They might buy a stock when it is low and sell it when it is high to earn a quick profit. This is similar to how Trading likes to exchange his stones quickly to earn more stones.

So, just like Investing and Trading, people have different strategies when it comes to the stock market. They can either invest for the long-term or trade for the short-term.

****

Once upon a time in the magical kingdom of Financia, there lived two fairies named Investor and Trader. Investor was a patient and wise fairy who loved to collect shiny stones and jewels. She knew that if she waited patiently, these stones and jewels would become more valuable over time. Trader, on the other hand, was a quick and clever fairy who loved to play games of chance. She knew that if she made quick decisions, she could sometimes make a lot of stones and jewels quickly.

One day, Investor and Trader went to the castle of the king of Financia, who was holding a great feast. The king had a new game for all his guests to play, called "Stock Market". He explained that the Stock Market was a place where people could buy and sell little pieces of ownership in big companies. Sometimes, these pieces of ownership would become more valuable over time, like Investor's shiny stones and jewels. Other times, they could become less valuable, like Trader's games of chance.

Investor thought the Stock Market sounded like a good way to collect more shiny stones and jewels over time. She decided to buy some of the little pieces of ownership in a big company she believed would do well. Trader, on the other hand, thought the Stock Market sounded like a fun game of chance. She decided to buy and sell the little pieces of ownership quickly, trying to make as many stones and jewels as possible in a short amount of time.

Over time, Investor's little pieces of ownership grew more valuable, and she was able to collect many more shiny stones and jewels. Trader, on the other hand, sometimes made stones and jewels quickly, but other times lost them just as fast. She never knew what would happen next, and sometimes found herself with fewer stones and jewels than she started with.

The difference between Investor and Trader is that Investor is like a patient gardener who plants a seed and waits for it to grow into a beautiful flower, while Trader is like a butterfly who flits quickly from one flower to another, never staying in one place long enough to see it grow. Both Investor and Trader can make stones and jewels in the Stock Market, but Investor is more likely to make them over time, while Trader's success is based more on chance.

A real-world example of investing versus trading in the Stock Market might be if someone bought little pieces of ownership in a big company like Apple and held onto them for many years, watching them grow more valuable over time, like Investor. On the other hand, someone else might buy and sell little pieces of ownership in Apple quickly, hoping to make stones and jewels quickly, like Trader. Sometimes the trader might make a lot of stones and jewels quickly, but other times they might lose them just as fast. It's up to each fairy to decide which approach is right for them.

※※※※※※※※※※※※※※※※※※※

Once upon a time, there was a magical kingdom ruled by the Fairy Queen. The Fairy Queen loved to collect magical items, like precious stones and rare flowers, and she had a group of fairies who helped her find these items.

One day, two fairies named Lily and Rose came up with different ideas on how to help the Fairy Queen. Lily wanted to search for new and rare items in faraway lands and bring them back to the Fairy Queen, hoping to make her happy with new discoveries. Rose, on the other hand, wanted to trade the magical items they already had for other rare items that were needed by the Fairy Queen's kingdom.

Lily loved the adventure and excitement of traveling to new lands, but Rose thought it was too risky and preferred to stay close to home. Lily's plan was called trading and Rose's plan was called investing.

The Fairy Queen knew that both plans had their advantages and disadvantages. Trading could bring in new and needed items quickly, but there was always a risk that they would not get as much as they hoped for when they traded. Investing meant they could hold onto their magical items for longer and hope they would become even more valuable, but there was always a chance they would not increase in value and they would miss out on other opportunities.

In the end, the Fairy Queen decided to use both strategies. She instructed Lily to continue searching for new and rare items in faraway lands, and Rose to trade some of their current items for other rare items that were needed by the kingdom. This way, they could maximize their gains and minimize their risks.

Just like the Fairy Queen, some people choose to invest their money for the long term, hoping it will increase in value over time, while others choose to trade in the stock market and buy and sell stocks quickly to make a profit. Both strategies have their advantages and disadvantages, and it is important to understand the risks and rewards of each strategy before deciding which one to use.

A real-world example of investing in the stock market is buying shares of a company that is expected to grow and hold onto them for a long time, hoping they will increase in value. A real-world example of trading in the stock market is buying and selling shares of a company quickly to make a profit based on changes in the stock price.

Merits and demerits of investing in stock market

Once upon a time, there was a fairy named Ella who loved to collect shiny stones. One day, she heard about a shiny stone market where she could buy and sell her precious stones. She decided to visit the market to learn more about it.

At the market, Ella met two fairies named Lily and Daisy. Lily told Ella that investing in the shiny stone market was like planting a seed in the ground and watching it grow into a beautiful flower over time. She said that investing meant buying a stone and keeping it for a long time, like a treasure, hoping that it would grow in value over time.

Daisy, on the other hand, said that trading in the market was like playing a game of catch. You buy a stone and sell it quickly, hoping to make a profit before the stone loses its shine. She said that trading was like a fun game, but it was risky and you could lose your money if you weren't careful.

Ella learned that investing in the market had many benefits. It could help her grow her wealth over time, and she could earn more money by buying and holding her stones for a long time. But she also learned that investing was not without its risks. The value of her stones could go up and down, and she might lose money if she didn't choose her stones wisely.

On the other hand, trading had the potential for quick profits, but it was also very risky. Daisy told Ella that she could make a lot of money quickly, but she could also lose it just as fast. It was important to be careful and make smart decisions when trading.

Ella realized that there were merits and demerits to both investing and trading. She decided to take her time and learn more before making any decisions. She knew that investing could help her grow her wealth over time, but it required patience and careful planning. On the other hand, trading could be fun and exciting, but it required a lot of knowledge and skill to be successful.

In the end, Ella learned that both investing and trading in the shiny stone market had their advantages and disadvantages. It was up to her to decide which path was right for her, based on her goals and risk tolerance.

Real-world example: Just like Ella, many people have to decide whether they want to invest or trade in the stock market. Investing in the stock market can help people grow their wealth over time, but it requires patience and careful planning. On the other hand, trading can be exciting and potentially profitable, but it's also very risky and requires a lot of knowledge and skill. People need to weigh the merits and demerits of both approaches and decide which one is best for their individual circumstances.

****

Once upon a time, in the magical kingdom of Fairytale Land, there were two fairies named Lily and Daisy. Lily loved to invest her fairy coins in the stock market, while Daisy preferred to keep all her coins in her fairy purse.

One day, Lily decided to explain to Daisy the merits and demerits of investing in the stock market. She said, "Daisy, by investing in the stock market, I can buy shares of a company that I believe will grow in the future. When the company grows, the value of my shares will also grow, and I can sell them for more fairy coins than what I paid for them. This is called a profit, and it can make me very wealthy in the long term."

Daisy was impressed, but she asked, "But Lily, what if the company doesn't grow as you expected? Won't you lose your fairy coins?"

Lily replied, "Yes, that's the demerit of investing in the stock market. The value of my shares can go down as well as up, depending on how the company performs. If the company doesn't grow, the value of my shares will also go down, and I may have to sell them for less than what I paid for them. This is called a loss, and it can make me lose my fairy coins."

Daisy understood and asked, "Can you give me a real-world example, Lily?"

Lily said, "Sure, let's say I invested my fairy coins in a company that makes fairy wands. If the company grows and becomes very popular, the value of my shares will also grow, and I can sell them for more fairy coins. But if the company is not doing well and people stop buying fairy wands, the value of my shares will go down, and I may have to sell them for less than what I paid for them."

Daisy nodded and said, "I understand now, Lily. Investing in the stock market can make you very rich, but it can also make you lose your fairy coins. You have to be careful and choose the right companies to invest in."

Lily smiled and said, "Exactly, Daisy. It's all about balancing the risks and rewards of investing. With a little bit of research and a lot of fairy luck, we can make smart investment decisions and grow our fairy coins over time."

****

Once upon a time, there were two fairy sisters, Lulu and Mimi. They both wanted to earn some fairy coins to buy new fairy dresses and jewelry. Lulu decided to invest her fairy coins in a fairy bank where she could earn interest over time. Mimi, on the other hand, decided to trade her fairy coins by buying and selling different fairy items in the fairy market.

Lulu's investment in the fairy bank paid off as she earned more fairy coins over time due to the interest she received. She was patient and didn't mind waiting a little longer to see her fairy coins grow. However, Mimi's trading strategy was riskier. She made some profits by buying low and selling high, but she also lost some fairy coins when she made bad trades. She was impatient and wanted to make quick profits.

In the end, Lulu had more fairy coins than Mimi because her investment strategy was more stable and long-term. Mimi learned that trading can be risky and requires a lot of skill and knowledge.

In the real world, people can invest in the stock market by buying stocks of different companies and holding onto them for a long time to earn a return on their investment. This is similar to Lulu's investment strategy. However, people can also trade stocks by buying and selling them quickly to make a profit. This is similar to Mimi's trading strategy. While trading can be profitable, it can also be risky and requires a lot of knowledge and skill.

****

Once upon a time in a magical land, there were two fairies named Flicker and Twinkle. Flicker liked to invest her fairy dust in a special tree that produced magic apples. She knew that if she waited patiently, her apples would grow and become more valuable over time. Twinkle, on the other hand, liked to trade her fairy dust with other fairies for different things like flowers or crystals. She loved the excitement of getting something new right away.

One day, Flicker and Twinkle met a wise old fairy named Sage. Sage explained to them the merits and demerits of investing and trading in the fairy stock market.

Flicker learned that investing her fairy dust in the magic apple tree had the merit of potentially earning her more fairy dust in the future. She also learned that investing required patience and that it was important to choose the right tree to invest in. However, there was a demerit to investing as well. The tree could get sick, and the magic apples could become less valuable. This would mean that Flicker would lose her fairy dust.

Twinkle learned that trading her fairy dust had the merit of instant gratification. She could get something new right away that she wanted or needed. However, she also learned that trading had a demerit. Sometimes, she would trade her fairy dust for something that turned out to be worth less than what she paid for it. This meant that Twinkle would lose her fairy dust.

Sage told Flicker and Twinkle that both investing and trading had their merits and demerits, and that they should think carefully about what they wanted to do. Sage also suggested that they could do both. Flicker could invest in the magic apple tree and trade some of her fairy dust for things she needed right away. Twinkle could trade her fairy dust but also invest some of it in something that might become more valuable over time.

Just like in the fairy world, in the real world, people can choose to invest or trade in the stock market. They need to consider the merits and demerits of each and decide what works best for them. For example, investing in a company's stock has the merit of potentially earning more money over time, but there is also the demerit that the stock could go down in value. Trading stocks has the merit of potentially earning quick profits, but it also has the demerit that people can lose money if they make bad trades.

✶✶✶✶✶✶✶✶✶✶✶✶✶✶✶✶✶✶✶✶✶✶

Once upon a time, there were two fairies named Luna and Nova. Luna was very smart and liked to think long-term, while Nova was very quick and liked to take risks. They both decided to try their hand at trading in the stock market.

Luna spent a lot of time researching different companies before she made any trades. She looked at their past performance, what they did, and how they made money. She only made trades when she was sure that the company was doing well and was likely to continue doing well in the future. This meant that Luna didn't make trades very often, but when she did, they were usually very successful. She was patient and her trades paid off in the long run.

Nova, on the other hand, was very impulsive. She didn't do any research and just made trades based on what she thought was going to happen in the market. Sometimes her trades were successful, but other times they weren't. Nova made a lot of trades and had a lot of excitement, but she also lost money more often than Luna did. She was impatient and her trades often didn't work out in the long run.

So, the merit of trading is that you can make money quickly and have a lot of excitement. However, the demerit is that it can be risky and you can lose money just as quickly as you can make it. It's important to do your research before making any trades and to think carefully before taking any risks.

In the real world, people trade in the stock market every day. Some people, like Luna, invest for the long term and are successful in the long run. Others, like Nova, make a lot of trades and hope to make a quick profit, but often lose money. It's important to know the risks and rewards before making any decisions.

Dividend in stock market

Once upon a time, in a magical forest, there lived a group of fairies who loved to play and have fun. One day, they decided to start a special game. They collected some seeds from their favorite plants and buried them in the ground. Over time, the seeds grew into beautiful flowers, and the fairies were so happy to see their plants thriving.

After a while, the fairies noticed that some of the flowers were growing bigger and stronger than others. They realized that the flowers that were getting more sunlight and water were growing faster. They decided to share the bigger flowers with each other as a reward for taking care of the plants.

This is kind of like what happens in the stock market when you buy a share of a company. When you buy a share, you become a part-owner of the company, just like how the fairies owned the flowers they grew. The company might use the money you invested to grow and make more profits, just like how the fairies used the sunlight and water to help their flowers grow.

And just like how the fairies shared the bigger flowers with each other, some companies share a part of their profits with their shareholders, and this is called a dividend. So, if you own a share of a company that pays dividends, you might get some extra money as a reward for being an owner of that company.

However, just like how some flowers don't grow as big and strong, sometimes companies don't do well and might not be able to pay dividends or even lose value, which means you could lose money if you sell your shares.

So, the dividend is a way for companies to reward their shareholders for their investment, but it's important to remember that investing in the stock market always comes with risks.

****

Once upon a time, in a magical land full of fairies, there was a fairy named Lily. Lily was very good at growing flowers and fruits, and she used to sell them in the market. One day, Lily decided to save some of the money she made and invest it in a fairy company that sold fairy dust.

The fairy company was very successful, and they earned a lot of money. At the end of the year, the company decided to give some of that money back to the fairy investors. This money was called a "dividend." When Lily received her dividend, she was very happy. She could use that money to buy more flower and fruit seeds to grow even more beautiful plants to sell in the market.

This is just like when you save your allowance and use it to buy a toy you really want. And if the company you invested in does well, they might give you some extra money, just like how Lily received a dividend. That extra money can help you save even more, or buy something else you've been wanting.

However, sometimes the company might not do well, and they might not give any dividends. This is a risk you take when you invest your money. But, if you choose a good company to invest in, and they do well, you might get a lot of extra money in return!

In the real world, many companies that are traded on the stock market pay dividends to their shareholders. For example, a company like Coca-Cola may pay a dividend to its shareholders, which is a portion of their profits. The shareholders can then use that money for whatever they want, just like Lily used her dividend to buy more flower and fruit seeds.

****

Once upon a time, in a magical forest far away, there were fairies who loved to plant flowers and take care of them. One day, the fairy queen decided to start a flower business and sell the beautiful flowers they grew to other fairies in the forest.

To do this, the fairy queen needed to raise money to buy more flowers and supplies. So she decided to sell a small part of her flower business to other fairies in exchange for some money. This way, the fairy queen could use the money to grow her business and make even more beautiful flowers.

As time went on, the fairy queen's flower business became more and more successful, and she started making a lot of money. But instead of keeping all the money for herself, she decided to share some of it with the fairies who had originally invested in her business.

This is called a dividend. It's like when you share your candy with your friends because they helped you make it. The fairy queen was sharing her profits with the fairies who helped her grow her business.

In the real world, many companies also give dividends to their shareholders. For example, let's say you invest in a company that makes toys. If the company is doing well and making a lot of money, they might decide to give some of that money back to their shareholders in the form of a dividend. This is a way for the company to thank their shareholders for investing in their business and to share their success with them.

Intra day trading in stock market

Once upon a time, in a magical forest, fairies loved to trade different kinds of things like acorns, berries, and flowers. One day, a group of fairies decided to try a new game called Intra-Day Trading.

In this game, the fairies had to quickly trade their items with each other in one day. The goal was to make a lot of trades and earn more items than they started with. The fairies were very excited to play this game, and they flew around the forest to start trading.

The first fairy had a basket of acorns, and she quickly traded them with another fairy for a bunch of berries. Then she traded the berries with another fairy for some flowers. This went on for the whole day, and the fairies made lots of trades.

At the end of the day, some fairies had more items than they started with, but some had less. The fairies who traded carefully and thoughtfully had more items, and the fairies who traded impulsively had less.

In the real world, grown-ups play a similar game called Intra-Day Trading in the stock market. Instead of acorns, berries, and flowers, they trade stocks of different companies, like Apple, Amazon, or Google. Just like the fairies, the goal is to buy and sell stocks quickly in one day to make a profit.

However, Intra-Day Trading is not always easy, and it can be risky because the value of stocks can change very quickly in one day. Sometimes, people can earn a lot of money, but sometimes, they can also lose a lot of money.

So, it's important to be careful and thoughtful when playing the game of Intra-Day Trading, just like the fairies in the magical forest.

****

Once upon a time in a magical land, there was a fairy named Flutter. Flutter loved to collect shiny crystals, and she knew that she could sell them to other fairies for more crystals. One day, she learned about something called intra day trading.

Flutter learned that intra day trading meant buying and selling the same crystals in one day. She could buy crystals when the price was low and sell them when the price was high, all in one day. She thought this sounded like a great idea, so she decided to give it a try.

At first, Flutter was excited because she made a lot of crystals quickly. But then she realized that sometimes the price of crystals would go down, and she would lose crystals. She also spent a lot of time watching the prices and worrying about when to buy and sell.

Flutter learned that intra day trading was very risky and could be stressful. She realized that she preferred to collect crystals and hold onto them for a long time, even if she didn't make as many crystals quickly.

In the real world, intra day trading is when people buy and sell stocks in the same day to try and make a quick profit. It can be risky and stressful, just like Flutter's experience with trading crystals. Some people enjoy the excitement of intra day trading, but others prefer to invest in stocks for the long-term and wait for their investment to grow over time.

✶✶✶✶✶✶✶✶✶✶✶✶✶✶✶✶✶✶✶✶

Once upon a time, there was a magical fairy kingdom where fairies loved to trade different things with each other. Some fairies had beautiful flowers, while others had sparkling gems, and some had delicious fruits.

One day, a group of fairies came up with a new idea of trading that involved trading things within a day. They called it "intra-day trading." The fairies would trade different things with each other, but they had to sell it by the end of the day. If they made a profit, they could keep the extra coins and buy more things, but if they didn't, they would lose their coins.

The fairy queen loved the idea of intra-day trading and encouraged all the fairies to try it. She explained that it was like playing a game where they had to be very quick and clever to make a profit. She also explained that it could be risky because they had to sell everything by the end of the day, even if they were losing coins.

For example, suppose a fairy had some beautiful flowers that they wanted to trade. In the morning, they could trade it with another fairy for some shiny gems. Then, in the afternoon, they could trade the gems with another fairy for some delicious fruits. Finally, they could sell the fruits to the last fairy and make a profit if they sold it at a higher price than what they paid for the flowers.

But the queen warned the fairies that they had to be careful not to keep the things for too long, or they might lose their chance to sell it at a good price. She also explained that sometimes the prices of things could go down, and they could end up losing their coins.

Just like in the fairy kingdom, grown-ups also trade things in the real world. Some people buy and sell things within a day, just like the fairies in intra-day trading. It can be exciting and profitable, but it can also be risky because prices can go up or down very quickly. So, it's essential to be careful and make wise decisions when trading in the stock market.

✱✱✱✱✱✱✱✱✱✱✱✱✱✱✱✱✱✱✱✱✱

Once upon a time, in a magical land, there were fairies who loved to trade things. One day, a fairy named Lily wanted to trade her shiny wand for a bag of fairy dust. She thought that she could trade her wand for the bag of fairy dust quickly and then trade the bag for something else that she really wanted.

So, she went to the Fairy Market, where all the fairies came to trade their things. Lily quickly found a fairy who was willing to trade her bag of fairy dust for her wand. Lily was so happy with her trade that she decided to keep trading.

She traded her bag of fairy dust for a pretty dress and then traded her dress for a big bag of marbles. She continued to trade and trade, and she was making a lot of trades in just one day!

In the evening, when she returned home, she was very happy with all her trades. However, when she looked at her bag of marbles, she realized that some of them were broken, and some of them were not as pretty as she thought they were. She also realized that she had lost some of the fairy dust she had traded earlier.

Lily learned that trading things quickly can be fun, but it can also have some problems. Sometimes things that seem valuable at first turn out to not be so valuable in the end. This is just like in the stock market when people do intra day trading.

In real life, intra day trading is when people buy and sell stocks within the same day. This can be exciting because you can make a lot of trades in a short amount of time, but it can also be risky because the value of the stocks can change very quickly, and you might end up losing money.

So, Lily learned that it's important to think carefully before making trades, just like in the stock market, and that it's okay to hold onto things for a little while to make sure they are really valuable to you.

Future and options in stock market

Once upon a time in the magical land of Far Far Away, there was a fairy named Fiona who loved to make deals with her fairy friends. One day, Fiona met her friend Tinkerbell who had a big bag of golden coins. Tinkerbell told Fiona that she wanted to sell her golden coins to her at a certain price, but the price of the coins might go up or down in the future.

Fiona thought about it and said, "I'm not sure if I want to buy your coins because I don't know if the price will go up or down." Tinkerbell replied, "Don't worry, Fiona. We can make a deal where you can buy the coins at today's price, and if the price goes up, you can buy the coins from me at today's price and then sell them to someone else at the higher price. If the price goes down, you don't have to buy the coins from me and you won't lose any money."

Fiona was intrigued and asked, "What is this kind of deal called?" Tinkerbell replied, "It's called a futures contract. You're basically buying the right to buy or sell something at a certain price in the future."

Fiona thought about it some more and said, "That sounds like a fun game to play, but is there anything else I can do with these futures contracts?" Tinkerbell replied, "Yes, you can also trade options. Options are like insurance policies that give you the right to buy or sell something at a certain price in the future. So, if the price goes up, you can exercise your option to buy at a lower price and sell it at a higher price. If the price goes down, you don't have to exercise your option and you won't lose any money."

Fiona was impressed and said, "That sounds like a really cool game to play. Can I buy these futures contracts and options from you?" Tinkerbell replied, "Sure, but remember that it's important to be careful when playing these games. They can be risky, and you can lose a lot of money if you're not careful."

Fiona thought about it some more and said, "I'll think about it. Maybe I'll just stick to buying and selling coins for now."

In the real world, futures and options contracts are commonly used by investors and traders to hedge against price movements and to speculate on the future price of commodities, currencies, and other financial instruments. For example, farmers might use futures contracts to lock in a certain price for their crops in the future, while investors might use options contracts to protect their portfolio against market volatility. However, futures and options trading can also be risky, and it's important to understand the potential risks before investing.

****

Once upon a time, there was a magical land of fairies called Fairyland. In Fairyland, there were two types of fairies: the Future Fairies and the Option Fairies.

The Future Fairies were very good at predicting what would happen in the future. They could see things that no one else could and knew when things were going to happen. The Option Fairies, on the other hand, had the power to choose different options and possibilities. They could see all the different paths that something could take.

One day, the King of Fairyland decided to build a new castle. He asked the Future Fairies when it would be finished, and they told him it would take three months. The King was very happy with this prediction, but he wanted to make sure he could finish it on time.

So, he went to the Option Fairies and asked for their help. They showed him all the different options he could take to finish the castle in three months. They suggested he could hire more workers, use better materials, or even build a smaller castle.

The King was amazed by all the options and possibilities the Option Fairies showed him. He decided to use some of their suggestions and finished the castle in just two months!

This is similar to how Future and Option trading works in the stock market. Just like the Future Fairies, people who trade futures predict what will happen in the future of the stock market. And like the Option Fairies, people who trade options have the power to choose different options and possibilities for their trades.

For example, let's say someone thinks that the stock of a company will go up in the future. They could use a futures contract to buy the stock at a set price and time in the future, which means they are betting that the stock will go up. Alternatively, they could use an options contract to have the option to buy the stock at a certain price in the future, but not necessarily have to do so, which gives them more flexibility and choice.

While trading futures and options can have potential benefits, it's important to remember that it can also be risky and is not suitable for everyone. It's always a good idea to talk to a financial advisor or do your research before making any decisions.

****

Once upon a time, in a magical land filled with fairies, there was a big field with lots of delicious fruits and vegetables. The fairies loved to eat these fruits and vegetables, but they were worried that the weather might not be good for growing them in the future.

One day, a wise old fairy came to them and said, "I have a way to make sure that you will always have enough fruits and vegetables to eat, no matter what the weather is like." She explained to them about futures and options.

"Futures are like a promise to buy something in the future, at a price that is decided today. So, we can make a deal with the farmers to buy their fruits and vegetables at a fixed price, even before they are grown. This way, even if the weather is bad and the prices go up, we will still be able to get our fruits and vegetables at the same price. And if the prices go down, we can still get them at the fixed price."

The fairies were impressed with this idea, but they still had some doubts. "What if we change our minds and don't want the fruits and vegetables anymore?" they asked.

The wise old fairy smiled and said, "That's where options come in. Options give us the right to buy or sell something at a fixed price in the future. So, if we change our minds and don't want the fruits and vegetables anymore, we can just sell our option to someone else who wants it. And if we really want the fruits and vegetables, we can exercise our option and buy them at the fixed price."

The fairies were very happy to hear this and they decided to use futures and options to ensure they always had enough fruits and vegetables to eat, no matter what the weather was like.

In the real world, farmers and food producers use futures and options to protect themselves from price fluctuations in the market. For example, a farmer might use futures to lock in a price for their crops, even before they are harvested. And a food producer might use options to protect themselves from rising prices of raw materials like sugar or wheat. This way, they can ensure a stable income or predictable costs, even if the market prices change.

****

Once upon a time, there was a group of fairies who loved to play games. One day, they discovered a new game called "Future and Options" in the enchanted forest. The game was about guessing the price of magical mushrooms that would grow in the future. Some fairies chose to buy the mushrooms at a certain price (called a "future"), while others chose to sell the mushrooms at a certain price (called an "option").

One fairy named Lily decided to buy a future for 10 magical mushrooms at a price of 5 gold coins each. Another fairy named Rose decided to sell an option for 20 magical mushrooms at a price of 4 gold coins each. They both believed that the price of the mushrooms would go up in the future.

As time passed, the mushrooms grew and their price changed. After a few days, the price of each magical mushroom went up to 6 gold coins. Lily was happy because she could now sell her 10 magical mushrooms for 6 gold coins each and make a profit of 10 gold coins. But Rose was not so happy because she had to buy 20 magical mushrooms at 6 gold coins each to fulfill her option, which cost her 120 gold coins, even though the market price was now 6 gold coins per mushroom.

This game of Future and Options was very similar to the real world, where people can buy and sell contracts for different items like stocks, commodities, and currencies. Like the magical mushrooms, the price of these items can change over time, and people can make money or lose money depending on their predictions and choices.

In the real world, people use futures and options to manage risks and make profits. For example, a farmer might sell a futures contract for his crop to lock in a price, so that he knows how much he will earn even if the market price goes down in the future. Similarly, a company might buy an option to protect against a rise in the price of a commodity that it needs for its business.

However, futures and options can also be risky, just like any other game. If you make the wrong prediction or take too much risk, you can lose money. It's important to understand the rules of the game and the risks involved before playing.

****

Once upon a time, in a magical land, there were fairies who loved to play a game called "Future and Options". In this game, the fairies would make a bet on the future price of magical berries.

One day, a fairy named Lily bought an option to buy 10 magical berries from her friend Rose at a future date for a price of 5 gold coins each. She paid a small fee to Rose for this option, but she knew that if the price of berries went up, she could make a profit. This was like buying a ticket to a future berry sale, but without the obligation to actually buy the berries.

On the other hand, Rose took on the obligation to sell the 10 berries to Lily for 5 gold coins each on the future date. She received a fee for taking on this obligation, but she knew that if the price of berries went down, she could lose money. This was like agreeing to sell a ticket to a future berry sale at a fixed price, but without knowing the actual market price of berries on the sale date.

As the days went by, the price of magical berries started to rise, and Lily realized that she could make a profit by buying the berries from Rose at the lower price that they agreed upon. She exercised her option, and bought the 10 magical berries from Rose for 5 gold coins each. She then sold the berries in the market for a higher price, and made a profit.

However, if the price of berries had gone down, Lily would not have exercised her option, and Rose would have made a profit by keeping the fee that Lily paid her.

In the real world, future and options are like bets that people make on the price of different things, such as stocks or commodities. They can be used to make a profit, but they also involve risks, and it's important to understand them before playing the game.

****

Once upon a time, in a land of fairies, there lived two fairy friends named Lily and Rose. Lily was a very patient fairy, and Rose was a very adventurous fairy. One day, Rose flew to the nearby town and saw a big building with many people coming in and out of it. She was very curious and wanted to know what was happening inside.

When she went inside, she saw people talking about something called "options and futures". She didn't understand what they meant, but she wanted to learn more. So she went back to Lily and asked her if she knew about it.

Lily explained to her that options and futures are like a magic spell that lets you buy or sell something in the future at a certain price. For example, imagine that you know a flower will bloom in the future and you want to buy it for a certain price. You can use an option or a future to lock in that price and make sure you can buy the flower when it blooms.

Rose thought it sounded amazing and wanted to try it. But Lily warned her that it can be risky because if the flower doesn't bloom, you might lose your money. Rose understood the risk and decided to try it anyway.

So, Rose used an option to buy the flower at a certain price, and Lily used a future to sell the flower at that same price. When the flower finally bloomed, Rose bought it at the agreed-upon price, and Lily sold it at that same price. They both made a profit!

But, if the flower had not bloomed, Rose would have lost her money and Lily would not have been able to sell the flower for the agreed-upon price, resulting in a loss for her as well.

The moral of the story is that while options and futures can be like magic spells, they can also be risky, and it's important to understand the risks before using them. It's always best to seek the advice of a trusted adult before making any decisions involving money.

Active return in stock market

Once upon a time, there was a fairy named Lily who loved to collect shiny, magical stones. She had a whole bunch of stones but wanted to make more. One day, she heard about a magical place called the Stock Market, where she could trade her stones with other fairies for even more stones!

Lily was excited and decided to visit the Stock Market. She met a fairy named Bella who told her about something called "active return." Bella explained that active return is like magic fairy dust that makes your stones grow bigger over time. But she also warned Lily that active return comes with some risks. Sometimes, your stones might shrink instead of growing.

Lily thought about it and decided to try her luck with active return. She traded some of her stones for special stones called "stocks" and "options." She learned that stocks were like long-term investments, and options were like short-term bets on which way the market would go.

Every day, Lily checked on her stocks and options. Some days they grew bigger, and she felt like the richest fairy in the land! But some days, they shrank, and she worried about losing her stones. That's when Bella reminded her about the risks of active return and how it's important to be patient and wait for the magic fairy dust to work its magic.

One day, Lily decided to sell her options and use the stones to buy more stocks. It was a risky move, but it paid off, and her stones grew bigger than ever before! She had successfully earned an "active return."

Lily was happy with her decision, but she also knew that there were risks involved with trading in the Stock Market. Sometimes the market can be unpredictable, and you may lose your stones. So, it's important to be careful and patient.

Just like Lily, some grown-up fairies invest in the stock market to grow their wealth over time, and some may choose to trade options to try to make quick profits. But they also have to be mindful of the risks involved and make informed decisions.

Real-world example: Just like fairies, people in the real world invest in stocks and trade options in the stock market. However, active return is a bit more complex and includes many factors like market volatility, economic conditions, and company performance. For example, if you invest in a company's stock, and the company performs well, the stock may grow, and you may earn an active return. But if the company performs poorly, the stock may shrink, and you may lose your investment. Similarly, if you trade options and predict the market's direction correctly, you may earn a profit, but if you get it wrong, you may lose your investment. Therefore, it's important to understand the risks and make informed decisions.

Demat account

Once upon a time, in a magical kingdom, there lived a little fairy named Lily. Lily loved collecting shiny stones and shells. One day, her friends told her about a special place where she could trade her stones and shells for other cool things like toys and books!

Excited about the opportunity, Lily went to the marketplace, but the shopkeeper told her she needed a special box to store her stones and shells, called a "demat box." The shopkeeper explained that the demat box would keep all of Lily's shiny treasures safe and secure, and she could easily trade them with others in the marketplace.

Lily didn't have a demat box yet, but she knew she needed one if she wanted to trade her treasures. She went to the fairy bank to open an account and get a demat box. The fairy bank gave her a special key to access her demat box and keep her treasures secure.

Now, every time Lily collected a new shiny stone or shell, she would put it in her demat box. She loved seeing her collection grow, and she knew she could trade her treasures whenever she wanted.

In the real world, a demat account is like Lily's demat box. It's a special account where people can store their investments in electronic form, like stocks and bonds. It keeps their investments safe and secure, and they can easily trade them with others in the stock market.

For example, let's say Lily's shiny stones and shells were actually stocks she bought from the stock market. She would keep them in her demat account just like she kept them in her demat box. When she wanted to sell her stocks, she could easily trade them with other investors who were interested in buying them.

So, just like Lily's demat box helped her trade her treasures, a demat account helps investors trade their investments in the stock market. It keeps their investments safe and secure, and makes it easy to buy and sell them whenever they want.

✵✵✵✵✵✵✵✵✵✵✵✵✵✵✵✵✵✵✵✵✵

Once upon a time, in a magical land called Dematia, there lived a young fairy named Daisy who loved to collect shiny objects. One day, Daisy met a wise old fairy who told her about a special type of shiny object called stocks. The old fairy explained that stocks are little pieces of ownership in companies, and if you own stocks in a company, you can make money if the company does well.

Daisy was very excited about the idea of owning stocks, but the old fairy told her that she needed a special kind of account to keep her stocks safe. This special account was called a Demat account.

The Demat account was like a magical storage box that kept track of all of Daisy's stocks. Whenever she bought or sold a stock, the Demat account would keep track of it and make sure she didn't lose anything.

Daisy decided to open a Demat account, and she put some of her shiny objects into stocks. She chose to buy stocks in a company that made fairy dust because she knew that many other fairies loved fairy dust and would always need more.

A few months later, Daisy checked her Demat account and saw that the value of her fairy dust company stocks had gone up!

This meant that her shiny objects were now worth more than before, and she could sell them for more money if she wanted to.

Daisy was happy that she had opened a Demat account and invested in stocks. She learned that even though it was important to keep her shiny objects safe, it was also important to use them wisely to make even more shiny objects in the future.

In the real world, people use Demat accounts to buy and sell stocks in companies. By investing in stocks, they can make money if the company does well and the stock price goes up. For example, if someone had bought stocks in Apple Inc. 10 years ago, their investment would have grown by over 1000% by now!

****

Once upon a time, there was a land called Stockmarketia, where fairies lived and traded stocks. In this land, there was a special kind of magic box called a Demat Box, which the fairies used to store their stocks.

One day, a little fairy named Lily wanted to buy a stock from her friend, but she didn't have any space in her magic box to store it. She asked her fairy godmother for help, who gave her a special key that would unlock a new magic box called a Demat Box.

The fairy godmother explained to Lily that the Demat Box was a very important box that helped fairies keep track of their stocks in a safe and secure way. The Demat Box worked like a fairy bank, where fairies could deposit their stocks and withdraw them whenever they needed.

Lily was very excited to use her new Demat Box and went to her friend to buy the stock she wanted. Her friend transferred the stock to Lily's Demat Box, and she was able to keep it safe and secure.

In the real world, a Demat Account is like a magic box that helps people keep track of their stocks in a safe and secure way. When people buy stocks, they receive them in their Demat Account, and when they sell them, they are transferred out of their Demat Account. It's like a bank account for stocks!

Just like how Lily's Demat Box helped her keep her stocks safe and secure, a Demat Account helps people keep their stocks safe and secure. It's a very important tool for anyone who wants to invest in the stock market.

****

Once upon a time, there was a fairy named Dotty who loved collecting precious gems and coins. One day, she heard about a magical marketplace where she could buy and sell these treasures with other fairies.

Excited to start trading, Dotty went to the marketplace and realized that instead of carrying her gems and coins in a bag, she needed a special container called a "Demat Account" to keep them safe and organized. This container was like a magical vault that kept track of all her treasures, so she could easily buy and sell them without worrying about losing anything.

Dotty quickly opened her Demat Account and was delighted to see that it came with a magical book called a "ledger" that recorded all her transactions. Whenever she bought or sold a gem or coin, the ledger would update automatically, keeping track of her precious treasures and the money she earned or spent.

Now, Dotty could easily trade her gems and coins with other fairies in the marketplace. She could buy new treasures that she loved and sell the ones she didn't want anymore. And with her Demat Account and ledger, she knew exactly how much money she had and where her treasures were at all times.

In the real world, a Demat Account works similarly for people who want to buy and sell shares in the stock market. Instead of gems and coins, they buy and sell shares of companies, and the Demat Account is like a secure container that holds these shares. The ledger keeps track of all their transactions, so they can easily buy and sell shares without worrying about keeping track of physical certificates.

Call Option in stock market

Once upon a time, in a magical kingdom far, far away, there was a brave knight named Sir Call. Sir Call was a very smart knight who loved to play games, especially one called "Call Option".

One day, the king of the kingdom came to Sir Call and asked for his help. The king had a lot of apples in his garden, but he didn't know what to do with them. Sir Call had an idea. He told the king that he would buy all the apples from him at a fixed price, but with one condition. Sir Call would pay the king a small amount of money as a promise that he would buy the apples at the fixed price, but Sir Call wouldn't actually buy the apples unless he needed them.

The king was a little confused, so Sir Call explained further. He told the king that he would keep the small amount of money as a token of his promise to buy the apples, and this token was called a "Call Option". If Sir Call ever wanted to buy the apples, he could use the Call Option to do so at the fixed price they agreed upon. But if Sir Call didn't want to buy the apples, he could just let the Call Option expire, and the king could keep the small amount of money.

The king was delighted with Sir Call's idea, and so they shook hands on the deal. Sir Call gave the king the small amount of money as a Call Option, and the king gave Sir Call the right to buy the apples at a fixed price in the future.

In the real world, people use Call Options to buy and sell stocks in the stock market. For example, let's say there is a company called "Apple Inc." that makes phones and computers. If you think that Apple Inc. is going to do well in the future, you can buy a Call Option that gives you the right to buy Apple Inc. stock at a fixed price in the future. If Apple Inc. does well and the stock price goes up, you can use your Call Option to buy the stock at the fixed price, and then sell it at the higher price to make a profit.

However, if Apple Inc. does not do well and the stock price goes down, you can just let the Call Option expire and you only lose the small amount of money you paid for the option, but you won't lose all of your money.

So that's the story of Sir Call and the Call Option. It's a way to make a promise to buy something in the future, but with the flexibility to not follow through on that promise if things don't go as planned.

****

Once upon a time, in a magical land far, far away, there was a fairy named Lily. She loved playing games with her fairy friends and one day, she came up with a new game called "The Call Option Game."

In this game, each fairy could buy a call option to a special magical crystal that was hidden somewhere in the forest. The fairy who bought the call option would have the right to purchase the crystal at a certain price, called the "strike price," within a certain time frame.

Now, let's say that Lily bought a call option for the magical crystal at a strike price of 10 fairy coins. A few days later, another fairy named Rose discovered the crystal and it turned out to be very valuable, worth 20 fairy coins. Lily was very happy because she had the right to buy the crystal at 10 fairy coins and sell it for 20 fairy coins, making a profit of 10 fairy coins.

In the real world, people play similar games with call options on stocks. Instead of buying a call option on a magical crystal, they buy a call option on a company's stock. If the stock price goes up, they can buy the stock at the strike price and sell it for a profit. For example, if someone bought a call option on a stock at a strike price of $50 and the stock price later rose to $100, they could buy the stock at $50 and sell it for $100, making a profit of $50.

So, just like Lily and her fairy friends played the Call Option Game with magical crystals, people in the real world play the Call Option Game with stocks. It's a way for them to make money by taking advantage of the ups and downs of the stock market.

****

Once upon a time in a magical kingdom, there was a wise fairy named Callie. Callie loved to play games, especially games that involved predicting the future. One day, she decided to play a game with her friends where they would try to predict the colors of the flowers that would bloom in the spring.

Callie had an idea. She offered her friends the chance to buy a magical flower card that would allow them to choose any flower color they wanted. Her friends were very excited about this opportunity and each bought a card.

As the spring approached, the fairies watched as the flowers began to bloom. Callie's friends were delighted to find that the flowers they had chosen were indeed the colors they had hoped for. They were able to enjoy the beautiful colors of their flowers all season long.

Callie had made a clever move by offering her friends the chance to buy the magical flower cards. She knew that some of her friends had inside information about which colors of flowers were going to bloom. By buying the cards, her friends were able to lock in their choices and benefit from the information they had.

In the stock market, there is a similar game that is played using a special card called a "call option." Just like Callie's magical flower cards, call options allow people to predict the future and make money. If someone thinks a stock is going to go up in price, they can buy a call option to lock in the price they will pay for that stock in the future. If the stock does indeed go up, they can buy it at the lower price they locked in with the call option, and then sell it for a profit.

For example, let's say someone buys a call option for 100 shares of a company's stock at a price of $50 per share. If the stock price goes up to $60 per share, they can use their call option to buy the stock at the $50 per share price they locked in, and then sell it for $60 per share, making a $10 per share profit.

Just like Callie's magical flower cards, call options can be a smart way to use information to make money. However, they can also be risky, as they expire after a certain period of time, and if the stock doesn't go up in price as predicted, the buyer of the call option can lose money. It's important to be careful when playing these games and to always seek the advice of a grown-up before making any investment decisions.

Put Option in stock market

Once upon a time in a magical kingdom, there was a fairy named Lily. She had a magical power to predict the future prices of a special kind of candy called "Fairy Berries". Everyone loved these candies and would buy them whenever they could. But sometimes, the price of Fairy Berries would go down, and people would lose money. This made Lily very sad, and she wanted to help.

One day, Lily learned about something called a "put option" that could help protect people from losing money if the price of Fairy Berries went down. A put option was like a magical contract that allowed someone to sell their Fairy Berries at a certain price, even if the price of Fairy Berries went down. This meant they could protect themselves from losing money if the price of Fairy Berries fell.

Lily went around the kingdom telling everyone about put options, and soon many people started using them to protect themselves. For example, there was a candy maker named Jack who had a lot of Fairy Berries that he needed to sell, but he was worried the price might fall. So, he bought a put option that allowed him to sell his Fairy Berries at a certain price, even if the price went down. This way, Jack was able to protect himself from losing money if the price of Fairy Berries fell.

Thanks to Lily's knowledge of put options, many people in the kingdom were able to protect themselves from losing money when the price of Fairy Berries went down. Lily was happy to see that her magic could help people, and she continued to use her powers to help others make smart choices in the stock market.

In the real world, put options work similarly to the magical contracts in the story. People can buy put options to protect themselves from losing money if the price of a stock or commodity falls. For example, if someone owns a lot of shares in a company and they're worried the price might go down, they can buy a put option that allows them to sell their shares at a certain price, even if the price falls. This way, they can protect themselves from losing money if the stock price drops.

****

Once upon a time, in a magical forest, there lived a kind fairy named Lily. She loved to help the animals in the forest and often used her magical powers to do so.

One day, a group of animals came to Lily, worried about their friend the squirrel. The squirrel had gathered many acorns for the winter, but he was afraid that their value might go down in the future. Lily listened carefully to their concerns and offered a solution called a "put option".

Lily explained that a put option was like a magic spell that would protect the value of the acorns even if their price went down in the future. She told the animals that they could buy the put option for a small fee, which would give them the right to sell the acorns at a certain price, even if their value decreased.

The animals were amazed by this idea and asked Lily how it worked. She explained that just like her magical powers, the put option gave them the power to control the future. If the value of the acorns went down, they could use their put option to sell them at the higher price they had agreed on, which would protect their savings.

The animals were delighted with this idea and asked Lily to help them buy put options for their own savings. Lily happily helped them, and the animals were able to protect their hard-earned acorns from any future price drops.

In the real world, put options work in a similar way. Investors can buy put options for a stock they own to protect themselves against a potential price drop. If the price of the stock falls, they can use the put option to sell the stock at a higher price and protect their savings. This is a way for investors to manage their risk and protect their investments from unforeseen events.

Blue Chip Stocks

Once upon a time, there was a magical land called Stockville, where fairies used to fly around with bags of gold coins. One day, the Queen Fairy announced that the fairies need to invest their gold coins to help Stockville grow and become even more magical. The fairies were excited and curious to know how they could invest their coins.

The Queen Fairy explained that they could invest in something called "Blue Chip Stocks." These were stocks of companies that were very strong and had a good reputation. The fairies knew that these companies were like the most popular fairies in Stockville - everyone knew them, and they were loved by everyone.

The Queen Fairy told the fairies that they should invest their gold coins in these companies because they were reliable and safe. These companies had been around for a long time, and they were not going anywhere. The fairies were excited to invest their gold coins in Blue Chip Stocks and help Stockville grow even more.

In the real world, Blue Chip Stocks are stocks of companies that have a good reputation and a long history of strong performance. These companies are usually leaders in their industry, and they are known for being stable and reliable. Examples of Blue Chip Stocks include companies like Apple, Microsoft, and Coca-Cola.

Just like the fairies in Stockville, investors in the real world invest in Blue Chip Stocks because they are considered safe and reliable investments. These stocks may not have the highest potential for growth, but they are less risky than other types of investments.

****

Once upon a time, in a magical land filled with unicorns and dragons, there was a wise fairy named Blue. Blue was known for her exceptional knowledge and had a special power to predict the future. One day, the queen of the land came to Blue and asked her to help her invest her gold coins. The queen wanted to invest her coins in the stock market and wanted to know which company's shares would be best to buy.

Blue knew just what to do. She suggested that the queen invest in Blue Chip Stocks. These were special companies that were known for being the best and the most stable companies in the land. They were like the strongest and most beautiful unicorns, always standing tall and strong, no matter what challenges they faced.

The queen was curious and asked Blue to tell her more about these Blue Chip Stocks. Blue explained that these were companies that had been around for a long time and had a strong reputation for being successful. They were like the most trusted and respected dragons in the land, who were always there to protect their people and never let them down.

Blue also told the queen that investing in Blue Chip Stocks was a smart choice because they had a strong track record of making profits and providing good returns to their investors. It was like having a magical fairy wand that always worked perfectly.

The queen was impressed and decided to invest her gold coins in Blue Chip Stocks. She saw her coins grow and her wealth increase steadily over time. She was grateful to Blue for her wise advice and thanked her for her help.

In the real world, Blue Chip Stocks are similar to the magical companies in this story. They are companies that have a long history of success and are considered to be the most stable and reliable investments in the stock market. For example, companies like Coca-Cola, Procter & Gamble, and Johnson & Johnson are often considered Blue Chip Stocks. People invest in them because they believe that these companies will continue to grow and make profits in the future.

****

Once upon a time, there was a kingdom ruled by a wise and wealthy king. The king had many treasures and jewels, but there was one special treasure that was the most precious of all. This treasure was a magic seed that could grow into a big and strong tree that would provide fruits and shelter for the kingdom.

The king decided to share this treasure with his people and asked his trusted advisors to find the most capable farmers who could plant and nurture the magic seed. After a long search, they found three skilled farmers who were given the task to take care of the magic seed.

The first farmer was very impatient and wanted quick results. He planted the seed in shallow soil and didn't water it properly, hoping that it would grow quickly. However, the seed didn't grow at all and withered away.

The second farmer was more patient and gave the seed a good start. He planted it in fertile soil and watered it regularly, and the tree began to grow slowly and steadily.

The third farmer was the wisest of them all. He knew that the magic seed was special and needed a lot of care and attention. He studied the soil, water, and weather conditions and made sure that the tree was well-nurtured. He even planted other trees around it to provide extra support and protection.

Years went by, and the magic tree grew strong and tall, providing shelter and food for the entire kingdom. The third farmer became very wealthy as he had taken care of the tree and sold its fruits and wood.

In the same way, there are some companies in the stock market that are like the magic tree. These companies are called Blue Chip Stocks. They are big and strong companies that have been around for a long time and are very valuable. Just like the magic tree, they need a lot of care and attention to grow strong and provide value to their shareholders.

For example, one real-world example of a blue-chip stock is Microsoft. It is a large and established company that has been around for many years and is known for its valuable products and services like Windows and Office. Investing in Blue Chip Stocks like Microsoft can be a good way to grow your money over time, just like the magic tree grew into a valuable asset for the kingdom.

Penny Stocks

Once upon a time, there was a young girl named Lily who loved to collect shiny stones. She would search far and wide to find the most unique and beautiful stones she could find. One day, while searching for stones in the woods, she stumbled upon a little gnome named Timmy.

Timmy was sitting by a small pond, looking very sad. Lily asked him why he was so sad, and Timmy explained that he had found a bag of gold coins, but they were all dirty and old. He wanted to use the gold coins to buy new shoes for his family, but he didn't know how to clean them or where to sell them.

Lily knew just what to do. She told Timmy that she had heard about a special market where people could buy and sell things, including old and dirty coins. This market was called the stock market, and there were even special kinds of coins called penny stocks that were sold there.

Penny stocks were like the gold coins Timmy had found, but they were not very valuable yet. However, if someone bought them and took care of them, they could become very valuable in the future.

Lily explained that some people like to buy penny stocks because they can be very cheap, but they can also be very risky. She told Timmy that if he wanted to sell his gold coins, he should clean them up and find a special person called a broker who could help him sell them in the stock market.

With Lily's help, Timmy was able to find a broker who helped him sell his gold coins for a fair price. He was able to buy new shoes for his family and even had some extra coins left over to buy Lily a beautiful shiny stone as a thank-you gift.

In the real world, penny stocks are stocks that trade for very low prices, usually under $5 per share. They are often issued by small companies that are just starting out and have not yet proven themselves in the market. While they can be cheap to buy, they can also be very risky and volatile, so it's important to do your research and be careful when investing in them.

****

Once upon a time, there was a kingdom where people loved to buy and sell things. They had a special place called the "stock market" where they could buy and sell tiny pieces of a company called "stocks."

One day, a fairy named Penny came to visit the kingdom. She was very small and had tiny wings, but she was very smart about money. The people in the kingdom loved to listen to her advice, so they asked her about something called "penny stocks."

Penny explained that penny stocks are like little pieces of a company that aren't very expensive. They might not be from big, well-known companies, but they can still be a good investment if you're careful.

Penny took the people to a little garden where she showed them some flowers. She said that some of the flowers were big and well-known, like roses and daisies, but others were small and not as well-known, like forget-me-nots and baby's breath.

She told them that penny stocks were like the forget-me-nots and baby's breath of the stock market. They might not be as famous, but they could still be very valuable if you took care of them and watched them grow.

One example of a real-world penny stock is a company called Sirius XM Holdings. They make music and entertainment for people to listen to in their cars. Their stock price is usually less than $10 per share, but if the company does well, the stock price could go up and people who own the stock could make a lot of money.

Remember, just like taking care of a flower, investing in penny stocks takes time and patience. But if you're careful and watchful, penny stocks can be a good way to make your money grow!

****

Once upon a time, there was a small village where everyone was busy with their work. In this village, there was a little girl named Lily who loved to save her pocket money. One day, her father told her about penny stocks in the stock market.

"Penny stocks are like magic beans, Lily," her father explained. "They may not look like much, but they have the potential to grow big and make you a lot of money."

Lily was intrigued. She imagined the penny stocks as tiny beans that she could plant and watch grow into a huge beanstalk that would reach the sky. But her father warned her that penny stocks were risky and could also shrink in value.

The next day, Lily decided to use some of her savings to buy a few penny stocks. She carefully selected some stocks that had the potential to grow and purchased them at a very low price. Lily waited patiently, watering her penny stocks like they were precious plants.

Over time, Lily's penny stocks grew and grew, just like the beanstalk in her imagination. They turned into real companies that made products and services people needed. As the companies grew, so did the value of Lily's penny stocks, and she made a profit when she sold them.

Lily learned that penny stocks were like little seeds that could grow into something big and valuable. She also learned that she had to be patient and do her research to make smart investments. Her father was proud of her for being a wise investor.

In the real world, companies like Amazon, Apple, and Google were once penny stocks that grew into huge, successful companies. Many investors, like Lily, saw the potential in these small companies and invested early, making a lot of money in the process.

****

Once upon a time, there was a little girl named Lily who loved to save her allowance money. One day, her friend Lucy told her about a way to invest her savings in something called penny stocks.

"Penny stocks are like little plants that can grow really big," Lucy explained. "You can buy them for just a few pennies each and then sell them later for more money!"

Lily was intrigued and asked Lucy how it worked. Lucy said, "Well, imagine you buy a seed for one penny, and then you plant it in your garden. If you take good care of it and the weather is nice, that seed can grow into a big beautiful flower that you can sell for lots of money!"

Lily understood that penny stocks were like little seeds that could grow into big flowers. She decided to invest some of her savings into a penny stock for a company that made toys. The stock was only worth a few cents, but Lily was hopeful that it would grow into something bigger.

A few weeks later, the company announced that they had made a new toy that was really popular. Lots of people wanted to buy it, and the stock price went up to 10 cents per share!

Lily was so excited to see her investment grow. She decided to sell her shares and made a profit of 10 times what she had originally invested! With her earnings, she bought a new toy for herself and saved the rest for her future.

In real life, penny stocks are stocks that are traded for very low prices, usually less than $5 per share. They are often for small or new companies that are trying to grow. While they can offer big returns, they can also be risky because they are more likely to go down in value. It's important to do your research before investing in any stock, including penny stocks.

Internal Rate of Return

Once upon a time, there was a little fairy named Twinkle. Twinkle loved to collect shiny things like gold coins, silver trinkets, and precious gems. She would often find these treasures hidden in the forest, or sometimes she would even trade with her fairy friends for them.

One day, Twinkle heard about a new way to make even more shiny things. It was called "Investing in Stocks". She was intrigued and wanted to learn more.

She flew to the wise old owl, who lived in a tree near the forest. The owl explained that investing in stocks meant buying tiny pieces of a company. The more pieces you buy, the more you own of the company. And if the company does well and makes lots of profits, the value of the pieces you own can go up too. This is called the "rate of return."

But then Twinkle asked, "What is the internal rate of return?"

The owl replied, "Ah, that's a bit more complicated. The internal rate of return is like a magic number that tells you how much money you will make over time from owning those little pieces of the company."

Twinkle was confused, so the owl continued. "Let's say you bought 10 pieces of a company for 1 gold coin each. And over time, the company made lots of money and the value of those 10 pieces went up to 2 gold coins each. If you sell them now, you would make a profit of 1 gold coin per piece. But what if the company also paid you a little bit of gold coins every year for owning those pieces? That's where the internal rate of return comes in. It helps you figure out how much profit you are making each year in addition to the profit from selling the pieces."

Twinkle was still a bit confused, so the owl gave her a real-world example. "Think of it like a fairy garden. You plant a tiny seed and over time, it grows into a beautiful flower. And every day, you water the flower and take care of it. That's like owning those little pieces of the company and getting a little bit of profit each year. And then, when the flower is fully grown, you can sell it for lots of gold coins. That's like selling those little pieces of the company for a profit too."

Twinkle finally understood and flew back to her fairy friends to tell them all about the magic of investing in stocks and the internal rate of return.

※※※※※※※※※※※※※※※※※※※※※

Once upon a time, there was a young prince named Jack who loved to play games. One day, he asked his fairy godmother to teach him a new game called "Investment Adventure."

The fairy godmother explained that the game involved buying and selling different kinds of magical beans, each with a different price. She told Jack that the price of the beans would change over time, and he could make a profit by buying the beans at a low price and selling them when the price was high.

Jack was excited to play the game, and he asked his fairy godmother how he could measure his success. The fairy godmother told him about a magical tool called the "Internal Rate of Return" (IRR) that would help him understand how much money he was making on his investments.

The IRR, she explained, was like a magic mirror that showed Jack how much he would earn if he kept his beans for a certain amount of time. If the IRR was high, it meant he was making a lot of money. If it was low, it meant he wasn't making much.

To help Jack understand, the fairy godmother gave him an example. She said that if Jack bought 100 beans for 10 gold coins each and sold them two years later for 20 gold coins each, his IRR would be 41%.

Jack was amazed, and he realized that the IRR was a powerful tool to help him make wise investment decisions. He thanked his fairy godmother and couldn't wait to play Investment Adventure.

And so, Jack learned the magic of Internal Rate of Return, and he used it to become a successful investor and live happily ever after.

****

Once upon a time, there was a fairy named Iris. She loved to collect magical seeds and plant them in her garden. One day, she found a special seed that had a sparkle like no other. Excited to see what would grow, she planted the seed and took care of it with love and patience.

As time passed, a beautiful tree grew from the seed. Its leaves shone in the sunlight, and the flowers on the branches were of many colors. Iris loved the tree so much that she decided to share it with her fairy friends. They came to admire the tree's beauty and were amazed by its size and strength.

Iris thought to herself, "I wonder how much this tree is worth in the human world." She decided to sell the tree to a human who would take care of it and appreciate its beauty. But how much should she sell it for? She couldn't decide.

So, she went to her friend, a wise old owl named Oliver, who knew all about the human world. Oliver told her that in the human world, they use something called the Internal Rate of Return (IRR) to calculate the value of investments like her magical tree.

Iris was confused, so Oliver explained it to her. "IRR tells us how much money we will earn on our investment over time, taking into account the amount of money we initially invested." He went on to say that the higher the IRR, the more valuable the investment.

Iris understood and was excited to know the IRR of her magical tree. She found out that the tree had an IRR of 20%. This meant that if she sold the tree for $100 today, in one year, she would have earned $20 from her investment. And if she kept the tree for five years, she would earn $100 in profit.

With this knowledge, Iris was able to sell her magical tree at a fair price to a human who appreciated its beauty and the investment potential. And as for the human who bought the tree, they enjoyed its beauty and watched it grow over the years, earning them a profit in the long run.

Real-world example: Just like Iris and her magical tree, people in the stock market use IRR to calculate the value of their investments. For example, a company may invest in a new project, and by using IRR, they can determine if the investment is worth it and will earn a profit over time.

****

Once upon a time, there was a farmer named Jack. He had a farm where he grew all kinds of fruits and vegetables. One day, Jack decided to plant some new crops on his farm, but he didn't have enough money to buy the seeds.

Jack had an idea to borrow some money from his friend, Tom, with the promise to pay back with interest after the harvest. Tom agreed and gave Jack $100 to buy the seeds. He told Jack that he would like to earn some interest on the money he had lent.

After the harvest, Jack earned a lot of money from selling his crops, and he paid back Tom $120. Tom was happy to receive more than he had lent, and Jack was happy to have a good harvest and make a profit.

Now, let's pretend that Jack and Tom were fairies living in a magical world. Jack wanted to plant some magical seeds that would grow into rare and valuable fruits that he could sell for a high price. However, he didn't have enough magic dust to buy the seeds.

Tom, being a wise and helpful fairy, offered to lend Jack the magic dust he needed to buy the seeds. But, Tom also wanted to earn some magic dust in return for lending his friend the money.

Jack agreed and promised to pay back the magic dust with extra magic dust after the harvest. When the harvest was over, Jack made a lot of magic dust from selling his rare and valuable fruits. He paid back Tom with even more magic dust than he had borrowed, and Tom was happy with the extra magic dust he had earned.

This is similar to how Internal Rate of Return (IRR) works in the stock market. When investors put money into a company or project, they expect to earn a return on their investment. IRR is the rate of return that an investor expects to earn from an investment over time. It helps investors decide whether an investment is worth their money and time.

For example, let's say a company wants to build a new factory, and they need $1,000,000 to fund the project. They decide to offer investors a chance to invest in the project, promising to pay them back with interest after the factory starts making a profit.

Investors may have different expectations for how much return they want to earn from the investment. Some may expect to earn a higher return, while others may be satisfied with a lower return. The company needs to determine the IRR that they can offer to attract enough investors to fund the project.

In this way, IRR helps companies and investors make informed decisions about investing their money in the stock market.

Extended Internal Rate of Return

Once upon a time, in a magical land, there was a wise old wizard named Wiz. Wiz loved to go on adventures and discover new things. One day, he stumbled upon a treasure chest filled with gold coins. He was excited to take the coins back to his castle, but he realized that some of the coins were cursed and would bring him bad luck.

Wiz wanted to figure out which coins were cursed and which ones were not. He knew that the cursed coins would bring him less wealth over time. That's when he remembered a magic spell called "Extended Internal Rate of Return" that could help him solve the problem.

Wiz cast the spell and it revealed which coins were cursed and which ones were not. He then sorted the coins and kept only the good ones, which would bring him more wealth over time.

In the real world, people use the "Extended Internal Rate of Return" to figure out which investments will bring them more money over time. It's like a magic spell that helps investors make better decisions about where to put their money. For example, if someone wants to invest in a company, they can use the Extended Internal Rate of Return to see if the investment will bring them a good return over time or not.

So, just like Wiz, investors use the Extended Internal Rate of Return to make wise decisions and find the right treasure that will bring them more wealth over time.

****

Meet Emma, a little girl who loves going to the beach with her family. One day, Emma's parents decided to buy a beach house. They had to take a loan from the bank to buy the house. However, they had a plan to rent out the house to other families when they weren't using it. This way, they could earn extra money to help pay off the loan.

Emma's parents wanted to make sure that they were making enough money from renting out the beach house to cover the loan payments and make a profit. They decided to calculate the Extended Internal Rate of Return (EIRR) of the beach house investment.

Now, let's break down what that means for a 4 year old:

Extended Internal Rate of Return (EIRR) is like a magic number that tells us how much money we will make from a long-term investment, like a beach house, after taking into account all the money we spend and all the money we make over a period of time. It helps us decide if the investment is worth it or not.

In this case, Emma's parents had to spend a lot of money to buy the beach house and pay for things like repairs, property taxes, and insurance. But they also made money by renting it out to other families. The EIRR calculation takes all of these things into account to give Emma's parents a clear picture of how much money they will make in the long run.

A high EIRR means that the investment will be profitable and a low EIRR means that the investment may not be worth it. In Emma's parents' case, they calculated a high EIRR which meant that the beach house investment was a good decision.

So, to summarize, the EIRR helps us figure out how much money we will make from an investment after taking into account all the money we spend and all the money we make over a period of time.

A real-world example of EIRR would be a company investing in a new factory. They would use EIRR to calculate the potential return on investment by taking into account all the costs involved, such as building the factory, buying equipment, and paying employees, and comparing it to the profits they expect to make from selling their products over the years. This calculation helps the company decide if it's worth investing in the new factory or not.

****

Once upon a time, there was a boy named Tom who loved collecting seashells at the beach. Every summer, he would spend hours searching for the most beautiful seashells to add to his collection. One day, he found a large seashell that was different from all the others. It was shiny and colorful, and he was excited to add it to his collection.

When he got home, he realized that the seashell was so valuable that he could sell it for a lot of money. He decided to hold onto it for a while and do some research to figure out the best time to sell it.

Tom learned about something called the Extended Internal Rate of Return, which is a way to figure out how much money he could make over time by holding onto the seashell and selling it later when it's worth more.

He discovered that if he held onto the seashell for a few years, it could be worth a lot more money. But he also learned that there was a risk involved because the value could go down instead of up.

Tom decided to take the risk and hold onto the seashell. He kept it safe and protected for several years, and when he finally sold it, he made a lot of money! He was able to buy a new bicycle, go on a vacation with his family, and even donate some money to his favorite charity.

So, the Extended Internal Rate of Return is like a magic crystal ball that helps you figure out if it's better to sell something now or wait and sell it later. It's important to do your research and understand the risks, but if you're patient and make the right decision, you can make a lot of money!

In the real world, people use the Extended Internal Rate of Return to decide whether to invest in things like stocks, real estate, and other assets. It helps them make informed decisions about when to buy and sell these assets to make the most money.

****

Once upon a time, there was a princess named Lily who lived in a castle. One day, her father, the king, gave her a magic box and told her that the box had a special power. He said, "Lily, this box will help you make wise decisions when you grow up and have to manage the kingdom."

The princess was curious and asked, "How can this box help me make wise decisions, father?"

The king smiled and said, "My dear, this is not an ordinary box. It has the power to show you how much money you will make from an investment. This will help you decide whether the investment is worth it or not."

The princess was amazed and asked, "How does it work, father?"

The king explained, "Whenever you want to make an investment, put the amount of money you want to invest in the box, and it will tell you how much money you will make in return. This way, you will be able to make wise decisions and manage your money well."

Years passed, and Princess Lily grew up and became the queen. She remembered her father's words and used the magic box to make wise decisions about investing in the kingdom's infrastructure, education, and healthcare.

One day, a group of merchants came to the kingdom and proposed a new business venture to the queen. They wanted to build a new market and promised to pay the queen a fixed amount of money every year for the next ten years.

The queen was intrigued but also cautious. She decided to use the magic box to calculate the investment's worth. She put the amount of money the merchants wanted to pay her every year in the box and found out that the investment was worth more than she expected.

However, the magic box also showed her another calculation called the Extended Internal Rate of Return (EIRR). The EIRR was a way to measure the investment's profitability by taking into account the time value of money, which means that money is worth more today than it will be in the future.

The queen realized that the EIRR was a better measure of the investment's worth and used it to make her final decision. She approved the investment, and the merchants built the new market, which became a bustling center of trade, bringing wealth and prosperity to the kingdom.

And that's how Princess Lily, the queen, used the magic box to make wise decisions and manage the kingdom's finances, including using the Extended Internal Rate of Return to measure the worth of investments.

****

Once upon a time, there was a farmer named Jack who lived on a beautiful farm with his family. One day, Jack decided to plant some new crops that he had never grown before. He had heard that these crops would grow really well and he could make a lot of money by selling them.

Jack worked hard to plant and take care of the crops. He spent a lot of money on seeds, fertilizers, and irrigation. Finally, the crops were ready to be harvested, and Jack was excited to see how much money he could make.

As Jack started to sell his crops, he realized that the prices were not as good as he had hoped. In fact, the prices were so low that Jack was barely making enough money to cover his expenses. Jack was disappointed and worried because he had spent so much money and time on the new crops.

But then Jack remembered something his friend had told him about the Extended Internal Rate of Return or EIRR. Jack learned that EIRR is a way to calculate how much money he would make from the crops over the long-term, taking into account the time and money he spent to grow the crops.

Jack decided to calculate the EIRR for his new crops, and to his surprise, he found out that he would actually make a lot of money in the long run. Jack was relieved and happy that he would be able to pay off his expenses and even have some extra money.

In the end, Jack learned that sometimes it's important to look beyond the immediate prices and take a long-term view to see the true value of his investments. Just like Jack, people in the stock market also use EIRR to calculate their investments and make better decisions.

Real world example: A company invests $100,000 in a new project and spends $10,000 each year for the next 5 years. After 5 years, the project generates $30,000 in profits each year for the next 5 years. By calculating the EIRR, the company can determine if the investment is worth the initial cost and annual expenses.

Stock Market Index

Once upon a time, there was a magical land called the Stock Market. In this land, there were many different types of fruits, like apples, oranges, and bananas. Some fruits were more special than others and people liked to keep track of how they were doing in the market.

To make it easier, they created a special fruit basket called the Stock Market Index. This basket was filled with the most popular and special fruits in the land, and people could use it to see how well the market was doing overall.

For example, imagine that the Stock Market Index had 100 apples, 50 oranges, and 25 bananas. If the value of the Index went up, it would mean that the prices of these fruits were generally going up, and if it went down, it would mean that the prices were generally going down.

In the real world, we have stock market indexes like the S&P 500, which is made up of 500 of the biggest and most successful companies in the United States. Investors use it to get an idea of how the stock market as a whole is performing.

****

Once upon a time, there were two friends named Jack and Jill. Jack loved to collect fruits and vegetables, and Jill loved to collect toys. One day, Jack came up with an idea to create a list of all the fruits and vegetables he had collected. He called it his "Fruit and

Vegetable Index" and it showed how many of each type of fruit or vegetable he had collected. Jill thought this was a great idea and decided to make her own index of toys.

A few weeks later, Jack and Jill were talking about how they could use their indexes to see which one of them had a larger collection overall. Jack said, "Why don't we add up all the fruits and vegetables and compare them to all the toys in your index?" Jill liked this idea and they did just that.

They found that Jack had 100 fruits and vegetables, and Jill had 50 toys. But they wanted to know more - they wanted to know how their collections compared to all the fruits and vegetables and toys in the world. So, they decided to do some research and see how many fruits and vegetables and toys were out there.

They discovered that there were millions of fruits and vegetables and toys all over the world! So, they realized that they needed a way to compare their collections to all the fruits and vegetables and toys in the world. That's when they learned about the "Fruit and Vegetable Index" and the "Toy Index" in the real world.

Just like Jack and Jill's indexes, the "Fruit and Vegetable Index" and "Toy Index" in the real world show how the stock market is doing by looking at a specific group of stocks. The stock market is like a giant collection of stocks from companies all over the world. And just like Jack and Jill's indexes, the "Stock Market Index" is a way to see how the overall stock market is doing.

For example, the Dow Jones Industrial Average is one of the most well-known stock market indexes in the world. It measures the performance of 30 large, publicly traded companies in the United States. If the Dow Jones goes up, it means that those 30 companies are doing well, and therefore, the overall stock market is doing well. But if it goes down, it means those companies are struggling, and the overall stock market is not doing as well.

So, just like how Jack and Jill used their indexes to see how their collections compared to all the fruits and vegetables and toys in the world, investors use the stock market index to see how the overall stock market is doing.

****

Once upon a time, there were many different stores in a big city. Each store sold different things, like toys, clothes, and food. One day, a group of people wanted to know how well all the stores in the city were doing, so they decided to count how much money each store was making.

They wrote down all the numbers and added them up, and that total number was called the "City Store Money Index". The index helped the people see if the stores in the city were making more or less money than before.

Now, let's say there was a store called "Toy World" in the city. The people who owned Toy World were very curious about how their store was doing compared to all the other stores in the city. So, they looked at the City Store Money Index and saw that it had gone up by 10% since the last time they checked.

They were happy to see that the stores in the city were making more money overall, and they hoped that their own store had also made more money. They checked their own sales and saw that their sales had gone up by 12%! That meant that Toy World was doing even better than the average store in the city.

This is kind of like the Stock Market Index in the stock market. Instead of counting the money made by stores, we count the value of different stocks. And just like Toy World, if a stock does better than the Stock Market Index, it means it's doing better than the average stock.

For example, the S&P 500 is a Stock Market Index that counts the value of the 500 biggest companies in the United States.

If a stock does better than the S&P 500, it means it's doing better than the average big company in the US.

Initial Public Offering

Once upon a time, there was a bakery called Yummy Treats. They made the most delicious cupcakes and cakes in the kingdom, and everyone loved them! One day, the owner of Yummy Treats, Mr. Baker, decided that he wanted to expand his business and open more bakeries all over the kingdom so that everyone could enjoy his treats.

But Mr. Baker needed a lot of money to do this, and he didn't have it all by himself. So, he decided to ask people to invest in his bakery and become a part-owner of the business. This is called an Initial Public Offering or IPO. Mr. Baker asked the king for permission to sell shares of his bakery to people in the kingdom.

The king agreed, and soon people started buying shares of Yummy Treats. Each share represented a small piece of the bakery, and when someone bought a share, they became a part-owner of the bakery. This meant that they would get a share of the profits that Yummy Treats made every year!

In no time, Yummy Treats had raised a lot of money from people all over the kingdom. With that money, Mr. Baker was able to open new bakeries in different parts of the kingdom. Now, people from all over could enjoy Yummy Treats' cupcakes and cakes!

In the stock market, an IPO is when a company, like Yummy Treats, sells its shares to the public for the first time. This allows people to invest in the company and become part-owners of the business. And just like how people who invested in Yummy Treats got a share of the profits, people who invest in a company through an IPO can also get a share of the company's profits if it does well.

A real-world example of an IPO is when Facebook, a popular social media company, went public in 2012. They sold shares of the company to the public for the first time, and people who bought those shares became part-owners of Facebook. Today, many people own Facebook shares and can earn a share of the company's profits if it does well.

****

Once upon a time, there was a boy named Tom who had a great idea for a lemonade stand. He wanted to sell his lemonade to more people, but he didn't have enough money to buy all the supplies he needed.

One day, a man named Mr. Smith came to Tom's house and said he wanted to help him turn his lemonade stand into a big business. He said he would give Tom a lot of money to buy everything he needed, but in return, he wanted to own part of the business. Tom was hesitant at first, but Mr. Smith explained that he was going to do something called an "Initial Public Offering" or "IPO" for short.

An IPO is when a company like Tom's lemonade stand decides to sell its ownership to the public for the first time. This means that people who want to invest in Tom's business can buy shares of ownership, called stocks, and become part owners too.

Tom thought it was a great idea because he could get the money he needed to start his business and people who believe in his lemonade could own a part of it too. Mr. Smith helped Tom prepare for the IPO, and soon Tom's lemonade stand became a big company with lots of people owning stocks in it.

Just like Tom's lemonade stand, many companies decide to do an IPO when they want to grow bigger and get more money to

235

invest in their business. A real-world example is when companies like Facebook and Uber did an IPO, and now people can own a part of those companies too.

Value stocks in stock market

Once upon a time, there was a little boy named Timmy who loved to collect shiny rocks. He had a special bag where he kept all his favorite rocks. One day, Timmy decided to trade some of his rocks with his friend Billy. Billy was very interested in one of Timmy's rocks, a plain-looking gray one, and offered to trade it for one of his shiny, colorful rocks. Timmy agreed, thinking it was a fair trade.

The next day, Timmy saw Billy with the plain gray rock he had traded, and it was now in a beautiful shiny case. Billy explained that he had taken the rock to a special store where they cleaned it and polished it until it shone like new. Timmy was surprised and a little sad that he had traded away something that could have been so valuable.

In the stock market, there are some companies that are like Timmy's gray rock - they may not look very interesting or exciting, but they can be very valuable. These companies are called "value stocks." Value stocks are companies that may be overlooked by investors because they are not the latest trendy company or industry, but they have solid financials and a proven track record of success.

One example of a value stock is Coca-Cola, a company that has been around for over 100 years and is known for its popular soft drink. While Coca-Cola may not be the newest or most exciting company, it has a long history of making profits and paying dividends to its shareholders. Investors who recognize the value of Coca-Cola and other similar companies can benefit from their steady growth and potential for long-term gains.

Just like Timmy learned that his plain gray rock could be valuable with the right care, investors can find value in stocks that may not seem exciting at first glance. It's important to do research and understand a company's financials before investing, but value stocks can be a smart choice for those looking for steady growth and long-term gains.

Small cap stocks

Once upon a time, there was a small town called Stockville. In this town, there were many different stores and shops, each selling different things. Some of the stores were very big and famous, like the supermarket and the toy store, but there were also many smaller stores that sold unique and special items.

One day, a new store opened up in Stockville. It was called "Small Cap Shop" and it was a very small store that sold handmade toys and crafts. The store was run by a woman named Sarah who was very passionate about her work and had a lot of love and care for each item she made.

The people of Stockville were very curious about this new store and many of them went to visit Sarah and see her beautiful creations. At first, only a few people bought things from her store, but as time went on, more and more people started to appreciate the quality and uniqueness of her items.

Soon, people from other towns started to hear about the Small Cap Shop and Sarah's amazing creations. They began to come to Stockville just to visit her store and buy her items. The store became very popular and successful, even though it was small compared to the other stores in town.

In the stock market, companies that are like the Small Cap Shop are called "small cap stocks". These are companies that are relatively small compared to other companies in the market, but have the potential to grow and become successful like the Small Cap Shop did.

Just like how Sarah's store started small and grew over time, small cap stocks may start small but have the potential to become big and successful if they are managed well and people appreciate their products or services.

A real-world example of a small cap stock is a company called Etsy. Etsy is an online marketplace where people can buy and sell handmade and unique items. When Etsy first started, it was a small website with only a few sellers and buyers. However, over time, more and more people started using Etsy and it became very popular. Today, Etsy is a publicly-traded company and one of the most successful small cap stocks in the market.

* *

Once upon a time, there were three little companies: the Big Company, the Medium Company, and the Small Company. The Big Company was very, very large and had lots and lots of money, while the Small Company was much smaller and didn't have as much money. The Medium Company was in the middle.

One day, the three companies decided to go to the stock market to get more money. The Big Company didn't need much money, so they only sold a few pieces of paper called "stocks". The Medium Company needed a bit more money, so they sold more stocks. But the Small Company needed a lot of money, so they sold many, many pieces of paper called "small cap stocks".

Many people wanted to buy the stocks of the Big and Medium Companies because they were very famous and successful. But not many people knew about the Small Company because it was still new and not many people had heard of it. So, the small cap stocks of the Small Company were very cheap, and people could buy lots of them for not much money.

Over time, the Small Company worked very hard and became more successful. More and more people heard about it and wanted to buy its stocks. As a result, the price of the small cap stocks went up and up and up! People who had bought the small cap stocks when they were cheap could sell them for a lot more money and make a lot of profit.

So, even though the Small Company was not as well-known as the Big and Medium Companies, it was able to give people a lot of money if they were willing to take a risk and invest in its small cap stocks. That's why small cap stocks are important in the stock market, because they can offer big rewards if the company becomes successful.

A real world example of a small cap stock is Roku, a company that makes streaming devices and provides TV streaming services. When Roku first went public and started selling its small cap stocks, not many people had heard of it. But now, many people use Roku to stream their favorite TV shows and movies, and the price of Roku's small cap stocks has gone up a lot, giving people who invested in them early a big reward!

****

Once upon a time, there was a big city with many different shops and businesses. Some of the businesses were very big and had lots of employees, while others were smaller and had only a few employees. The businesses that had only a few employees were called "small businesses."

Now, imagine that each of these businesses was like a toy car. The big businesses were like the big toy cars, and the small businesses were like the small toy cars. Just like the toy cars, each business has a price tag on it.

The price tag tells you how much it costs to buy the business. But here's the tricky part: just like the toy cars, the price of the businesses can go up and down, depending on how popular they are.

The businesses that have a lot of customers and make a lot of money are very popular, so their price goes up. These businesses are like the big toy cars. But the businesses that have fewer customers and make less money are not as popular, so their price stays low. These businesses are like the small toy cars.

The small businesses with low prices are called "small cap stocks" in the stock market. Investors might buy these small cap stocks because they think that the businesses might become more popular in the future and the price will go up. Just like when you buy a toy car hoping it will be worth more in the future.

For example, imagine a small business called "Bakery Bites" that makes delicious cupcakes. It only has a few employees, so it's a small business with a low price tag. But one day, a famous food critic visits Bakery Bites and writes a great review about their cupcakes. Suddenly, lots of people want to buy cupcakes from Bakery Bites, and the business becomes more popular. The price of Bakery Bites might go up, and investors who bought the small cap stocks might make some money.

So, in summary, small cap stocks are like small toy cars that have a lower price tag than big toy cars. Investors might buy them because they think the small businesses might become more popular and the price will go up, just like when you buy a toy car hoping it will be worth more in the future.

Mid - cap stocks

Once upon a time, there was a group of companies that wanted to grow bigger and stronger. These companies were already bigger than the little ones but not as big as the giants. They were like the middle children of the stock market family, and people called them "mid-cap" stocks.

Mid-cap stocks were companies that had been around for a while and had proven that they were good at making money. They had already grown a lot, but they still had room to grow even more. They were like teenagers who had grown a lot but still had more growing to do.

People liked mid-cap stocks because they had the potential to make a lot of money for their investors, but they were also a little bit risky. You see, because mid-cap companies were still growing, they had to take risks to keep growing. Sometimes those risks paid off, and sometimes they didn't.

But people who were willing to take a little bit of risk could buy mid-cap stocks and hopefully make a lot of money in the future. It was like planting a seed in the ground and watching it grow into a big tree over time.

A real-world example of a mid-cap stock is the company called Peloton. Peloton is a company that makes exercise equipment and has become really popular in the last few years. They're not as big as companies like Apple or Amazon, but they're bigger than some of the smaller companies you might not have heard of. Peloton has already grown a lot, but they still have room to grow even more, and some people think they could make a lot of money if they invest in Peloton's stock.

****

Once upon a time, there were some companies that were not very big, but not very small either. They were just the right size. They were called "Mid-cap" companies.

These companies were like the middle child in a family. They were not the oldest or the youngest, but somewhere in between. They had grown bigger than the small companies, but were not as big as the large ones.

Now, just like how children grow and become stronger and smarter, these mid-cap companies grew and became more successful over time. They had good ideas and worked hard to make their products and services better.

People who wanted to invest their money in the stock market, looked for these mid-cap companies because they had a lot of potential to become even more successful in the future. When people buy a little piece of these companies (called stocks), they could share in the profits that the companies make.

For example, let's say there is a mid-cap company called "Toys R Us". They sell toys and games to children and families. People who like this company might buy some of their stocks because they believe that the company will become even more popular and successful in the future.

So, just like how a middle child can grow up to be strong and successful, mid-cap companies can also become big and successful if they work hard and have good ideas.

****

Sure, here's another story to explain mid-cap stocks in the stock market:

Once upon a time, there were three friends who loved to play basketball. One was really tall and strong, one was average height and had good skills, and the other was short but very quick. They all dreamed of playing for their favorite basketball team, the Bluebirds.

One day, the Bluebirds announced that they were looking for new players to join their team. The tall friend thought he had the best chance of getting picked because he was the strongest, but the short friend thought his speed would be an advantage. The average-height friend didn't think he had any special qualities, but he decided to try anyway.

When they arrived at the tryouts, they saw that there were lots of other kids there too. Some were really tall and some were really fast, but most of them were about the same size and skill level as the three friends. The friends were worried they wouldn't stand out in the crowd.

But then they saw a sign that said the Bluebirds were looking for players who were "just right" - not too big or too small, but somewhere in the middle. They wanted players who had good skills and were ready to learn and grow with the team.

The average-height friend realized that he might have a better chance of getting picked than he thought. He wasn't the biggest or the fastest, but he had worked hard to improve his skills, and he was always willing to learn more. The other friends agreed and decided to give it their best shot.

In the end, all three friends were picked to join the Bluebirds. They were thrilled to be part of the team and excited to play in the big games ahead.

In the stock market, mid-cap stocks are like the average-height friend. They are not the biggest or the smallest companies, but they have a good balance of size, growth potential, and stability.

They may not be as well-known as the biggest companies, but they have the potential to grow and become even more successful. A real-world example of a mid-cap stock is Etsy, which is a company that operates an online marketplace for handmade and vintage goods. It is not as big as Amazon, but it has a strong brand and loyal customer base, and its stock has performed well over time.

****

Once upon a time, there was a boy named Timmy who loved to play with marbles. He had a small bag filled with different kinds of marbles that he would carry around with him everywhere he went. One day, his friend Billy asked to see Timmy's marbles.

As Timmy emptied his bag, he noticed that some of his marbles were smaller and some were bigger. He explained to Billy that the small marbles were worth less than the big marbles, but he still liked to keep them all together in his bag.

Just like Timmy's bag of marbles, the stock market has different types of companies with different sizes. Some companies are small, some are big, and some are in the middle. These are called small-cap, large-cap, and mid-cap companies.

Timmy explained to Billy that mid-cap companies were like the marbles in his bag that were not too big and not too small. They were just the right size. These companies were not as well-known as the big companies but were still strong and growing. They had the potential to become big one day.

Timmy told Billy about a real-world example of a mid-cap company called Etsy. Etsy is a company that allows people to buy and sell handmade and vintage items online. When Etsy first started, it was a small company, but now it has grown to become a mid-cap company. Many people use Etsy to buy and sell unique items, and the company continues to grow.

Billy understood now that mid-cap companies were like the marbles that were not too big and not too small, and that they had the potential to become big in the future. Timmy was happy that he could share his love of marbles and the stock market with his friend.

Large - cap stocks

Once upon a time, there was a giant named Biggie. He was the strongest and tallest giant in the land and everyone looked up to him. One day, Biggie decided to start his own business selling huge boulders to other giants. He knew that if he worked hard, he could make a lot of money and become very successful.

Biggie's business was doing very well and he became very famous among the giants. He hired other giants to help him and soon his business grew even bigger. Everyone wanted to buy boulders from Biggie because they knew he was the best.

As Biggie's business grew, he became very successful and he decided to sell his business to other giants. Because his business was so big and successful, it was worth a lot of money. The giants who bought his business became very rich too, because they now owned a big and successful business.

In the stock market, there are companies just like Biggie's business that are very big and successful. They're called large-cap stocks. When people invest in large-cap stocks, they're buying a small piece of that big and successful company. And if the company continues to grow and become even more successful, the value of those small pieces of the company will also go up, and the people who invested in them will make a lot of money.

A real-world example of a large-cap stock is Apple Inc. They're a very big and successful company that makes iPhones, iPads, and other electronics. Lots of people own a small piece of Apple by buying their stock, and because Apple continues to grow and become even more successful, the value of that stock goes up, making those people a lot of money.

****

Once upon a time, there was a big store in the city where people could buy all sorts of things like toys, clothes, and gadgets. This store was called the Big Store and it was very famous in the city.

One day, the owners of the Big Store decided that they wanted to make their store even bigger and better. They needed a lot of money to do this, so they decided to sell part of their store to other people who wanted to own a piece of it.

This is called an "initial public offering" or "IPO" for short. When the owners of the Big Store sold part of their store to the public, they got a lot of money in return. They used this money to make the store even bigger and better than before.

Now, when people wanted to buy things from the Big Store, they were not only customers, but also owners of a small part of the store. This made them feel proud and happy because they were part of something big and successful.

The part of the store that people could buy was called a "share". The owners of the Big Store decided to divide their store into many shares and sell them to the public. The people who bought the shares became owners of a small part of the Big Store.

Over time, the Big Store became even bigger and more successful, and the value of its shares went up. This made the people who owned shares very happy because the value of their shares had increased too.

This is what "large-cap stocks" are like in the stock market. Large-cap stocks are stocks of big and successful companies like the Big Store. When people buy shares of these companies and the companies become more successful, the value of their shares can go up too.

For example, if you buy a share of a company like Apple, which is a large-cap stock, and the company does well and becomes even more successful, the value of your share can go up too. This means you can sell your share for more money than you bought it for and make a profit!

SEBI

Once upon a time, there was a big playground where lots of children would come to play. There were swings, slides, and many other fun things to do. But sometimes, there were some children who would try to cheat or play unfair games, which would make others unhappy.

One day, some grown-ups came to the playground and set up a special area just for playing fair games. They called themselves the SEBI, which stands for Securities and Exchange Board of India. The SEBI made sure that all the games played in this area were fair and everyone had an equal chance to win.

The SEBI also made sure that the children who played in the fair games area followed certain rules, like not using any tricks or unfair means to win. They would keep a watchful eye on everything happening in the fair games area.

The SEBI also made sure that all the children who came to the playground were safe and not getting hurt while playing. They would check all the equipment and make sure everything was in good condition.

In the real world, the SEBI is an organization that makes sure that the stock market is fair and transparent. It makes sure that companies who want to sell their shares to the public follow certain rules and regulations so that people who invest their money in these companies are not cheated. The SEBI also makes sure that the stock market is safe and stable, just like the playground that was made safe and stable by the grown-ups.

For example, imagine a company wants to sell its shares to the public for the first time. The SEBI would make sure that the company follows all the rules and regulations and provides all the necessary information to the public so that people can make informed decisions before investing their money. The SEBI would also make sure that the stock market is safe and stable, just like the playground was made safe and stable by the grown-ups.

****

Once upon a time, there was a very important person named SEBI. He had a very important job in the stock market. His job was to make sure that everyone played by the rules.

You see, in the stock market, people buy and sell things called "stocks" which represent a part of a company. It's kind of like buying a piece of candy from a candy store. But sometimes, people don't play fair in the stock market. They might try to trick others into buying bad stocks or they might lie about how much a company is really worth.

That's where SEBI comes in. His job is to make sure that everyone is honest and follows the rules. He makes sure that people tell the truth about the companies they are selling stocks for and that they don't cheat anyone.

SEBI also helps to protect the people who buy stocks. He makes sure that the companies that sell stocks are safe and trustworthy. That way, people can feel confident that they are making a good choice when they buy a stock.

SEBI works very hard to make sure that the stock market is a fair and honest place. That way, everyone can feel good about buying and selling stocks and everyone can be successful.

For example, let's say there is a company that wants to sell stocks to people. Before they can do that, they need to follow some rules that SEBI has made. They need to give honest information about how their company is doing and how much it's worth. This way, people who want to buy the company's stocks can make a good decision about whether or not to buy them. If the company tries to cheat or lie, SEBI will catch them and make sure they get in trouble.

Afterword

Congratulations on completing "Stock Market as Bedtime Stories." I hope you enjoyed the book and found it to be informative, engaging, and entertaining. In this afterword, I want to share with you some additional thoughts on the importance of financial education and the role that this book can play in your journey towards financial literacy.

Financial literacy is a critical life skill that is often overlooked in our education system. It is estimated that nearly two-thirds of Americans lack basic financial knowledge, and this lack of knowledge can have significant long-term consequences. Without a basic understanding of finance, it can be challenging to make informed decisions about investments, savings, and debt management.

Fortunately, it is never too late to start learning about finance. And the earlier you start, the better off you will be. This is where "Stock Market as Bedtime Stories" comes in. The book is an excellent resource for anyone who wants to learn about the stock market and investing in a fun and engaging way.

The stories in this book are designed to make complex financial concepts accessible and easy to understand. Through engaging tales and relatable characters, the book teaches important lessons about the stock market and investing that will be valuable for a lifetime. By reading these stories, children can develop a foundation of financial knowledge that will serve them well throughout their lives.

But this book is not just for children. Adults can also benefit from reading these stories. If you are new to investing or looking to improve your financial literacy, "Stock Market as Bedtime Stories" is an excellent place to start. The stories in this book cover a range of topics, from the basics of the stock market to more advanced concepts like diversification and risk management. Whether you are a beginner or an experienced investor, there is something in this book for everyone.

One of the things I appreciate most about this book is its emphasis on the importance of investing in oneself. The characters in these stories are curious, motivated, and always seeking to improve themselves. They understand that investing in their knowledge and skills is the key to long-term success. This is a lesson that is as relevant to adults as it is to children.

In conclusion, I want to thank the author for creating this wonderful book. "Stock Market as Bedtime Stories" is an excellent resource for anyone who wants to learn about finance in a fun and engaging way. I believe that this book has the potential to inspire a new generation of investors and help to close the financial literacy gap that exists in our society.

I encourage you to share this book with your friends and family members. By spreading the word about the importance of financial education, we can help to create a more financially literate society. And who knows? Maybe one day, one of the children who reads this book will become the next Warren Buffett.

Happy investing!

www.ingramcontent.com/pod-product-compliance
Lightning Source LLC
Chambersburg PA
CBHW031532210526
45464CB00020B/1570